SOMETHING UNSEEN

By Stephen Hill

An Old Line Publishing Book

Printed in the United States of America

ISBN-13: 978-0-9846143-4-9
ISBN-10: 0-9846143-4-6

This book is based on a true story. Most references to real people, events, establishments, organizations, or locales have been changed or altered to provide a semblance of privacy yet keep a sense of authenticity.

Cover Design by Misty Dawn
Editing Services by Rebecca Vickery
Author Photo by Sandy Harrington

Old Line Publishing, LLC
P.O. Box 624
Hampstead, MD 21074
Toll-Free Phone: 1-877-866-8820
Toll-Free Fax: 1-877-778-3756
Email: oldlinepublishing@comcast.net
Website: www.oldlinepublishingllc.com

DEDICATION

To my loving wife, Rebecca Lynn

Something Unseen

CHAPTER ONE

There is an old saying that dates back from the pirate days and I have heard it many times throughout my life. *Dead men tell no tales.* I always thought this saying to be logical and true. That is—until the day I accidentally discovered that sometimes they can and do. Speak—I mean. I didn't believe it myself at first, so I'll understand if you choose not to believe me now. If you think me insane, then its okay, you won‘t be the first. At times I thought so myself. But I want you to know every word is true and it just might change your outlook on life—and death. Just as it has forever changed mine.

I was raised in the Presbyterian faith. Brought up in a God fearing, Christian home. Sunday mornings would find me in church school and then the eleven o'clock worship service. My family never missed a service as long as I can remember.

Our Pastor taught us that one day we shall all be judged. Our thoughts and deeds in this life will determine our eternal fate. Walk the righteous path and seek the Lord and your reward will be everlasting life. Stray from the path and seek earthly pleasures and your punishment will be eternal damnation in the fires of hell. There is nothing in between. Your soul is either accepted into heaven or it is banished into the pit. Your choice, choose wisely. This is what I was taught to believe... And I did for the first fifty years of my life.

Now, what if I told you this was not exactly the case? That there is an *in-between*, a place filled with restless souls who are either lost or trapped in some unseen realm. A place, neither heaven nor hell in the Biblical sense, but a living hell for the souls dwelling there. Crazy? Well, maybe... What if I told you I have proof?

I said my discovery was by accident, but now as I think back on the events of that day I have my doubts. Another old saying I think may apply here, *everything happens for a reason.* Although I didn't realize it at the time, I cannot help but believe now this adage holds some truth. At least in my case it seems so.

What else could possibly explain the chain of events that would lead me down the path I now tread? It is a dark path. Where it may take me, I do not know. I only know I am meant to follow to its end, wherever that might be. So, was it by design I found myself filming headstones in a cemetery on a cool September morning? Or did I blindly stumble into something that will haunt me for eternity?

~~~~~~~

"Be back in an hour, Hon," I shouted as I went out the front door. I was in a great mood that fine Saturday. My back was not aching as bad as usual in the morning and I purchased a new camcorder the evening before. I stayed up late reading the manuals and, like a kid with a new toy, I couldn't wait to try it out. Lord knows I needed to get out of the house for a change. An injury at work and the resulting surgery had put me out of commission for months. Boredom seemed to be the norm lately. If I didn't have my
~~~~~~~

research to keep my mind occupied I surely would have gone mad.

The internet is a wonderful source of information on practically any subject you can think of. My subject of interest happened to be the American Civil War. I spent countless hours online, reading about the battles fought by brave men who were willing to kill and die for a cause. I found it to be very interesting subject matter, especially the letters sent home from the battlefields. Those letters lend a brief glimpse into the personal lives of the soldiers who wrote them; a glimpse back in time, if you will. What started as a way to pass the long hours of my recovery became a fascination. Something to keep my mind off the pain and frustration I felt since my injury occurred. I decided to take my research a step further.

Someone mentioned there were Confederate gravesites in the cemetery at my church. I wanted to learn more about these soldiers who lived here in my hometown and fought and died for their beliefs. What company and unit they belonged to and which battles ended their young lives. I had no way of knowing then, as I stood filming their gravestones with my new camera, that this simple act would change me forever.

Pvt. Bradley Brown, Company C, 8th Battalion N.C. , Pvt. John Pleasents, Company H, 5th Battalion N.C. These were the names clearly etched in the government issued stone markers I recorded on film. I carefully wrote down the information from each headstone on the short clip, pleased at how clear the tape turned out.

"Come in here and check this out!" I called to my wife, who was in the kitchen cleaning up after lunch. "Wow, this camera is great," I exclaimed.

We both marveled at the clarity of the picture and sound quality. There was one stone on the film that did not have the company and battalion listed. I found it to be the most interesting. The stone marked the final resting place of two brothers, Jacob and

Jubel Pharr. The inscription listed the names then went on to say they were soldiers of the C.S.A. and they were killed in action.

I noticed these graves had no government headstone like the others. It was just an ordinary tombstone that had fallen over at some point in time. I can still feel the sadness that suddenly swept over me as I was standing by the grave. Why no military markers to honor these brothers in arms? Why were they buried in the same grave? It is still a mystery to me now, just as it was on that morning three years ago. However, I was soon to learn this was not the only mystery my camera documented in the graveyard that day.

~~~~~~~

I listened to the voice a hundred times during the past few hours. How did it get on the audio of my camera footage? It was definitely there! A faint voice, just a whisper, but it caused me to sit there listening with my mouth agape in disbelief. I was certain I was the only living soul in the cemetery that morning. No one could have gotten close enough to whisper into the camera without my knowing it.

This realization caused the hair on the back of my neck to stand on end. What on earth could have caused this to be there? Whatever it was would have been right next to me! Ghostly voices from beyond the grave? Caught on tape? I had read about that once somewhere, but dismissed it as fiction, or fantasy. After all, *dead men tell no tales*. The phenomenon is called EVP, which stands for Electronic Voice Phenomena. EVP is a voice or sound not heard at the time it was recorded. It is audible, however, upon playback of the recording. The article stated some researchers believe these voices to be those of the dead. *What a load of crap*, I remember thinking at the time I read it. But now, I wasn't so sure. I had no other explanation for the voice. None that made any more sense than the EVP theory.
~~~~~~~

Why did this voice speak to me, if it was in fact speaking to me? And why did it say what was recorded on the tape from my camera? I lay awake until the early hours of the morning pondering these questions. I finally drifted off to sleep with the whisper still playing over and over in my head. "Pray... Pray for me." The only thing I knew for certain was I just found a new course of study. Or... Had it found me?

CHAPTER TWO

"Steve... Stephen! I'm home," my wife shouted down the dark hallway. Hearing no reply, she proceeded down the corridor and opened the door to my office. "Steve?"

I hadn't heard her and the sight of her standing there gave me quite a start.

"What are you doing, honey?" she asked.

"Just some research, dear," I replied.

"With your headphones on?" she inquired. "No wonder you didn't hear me. How did physical therapy go today?" she wanted to know.

"Shoot, was that today?" I completely forgot about it. There had been other things on my mind lately. Things I didn't want to discuss with her. Not just yet anyway. Not until I had more answers. She had enough worries as it was and I didn't want my sanity to become one of them. So I thought it best not to mention what I really had done that day while she was at work. And besides, I didn't lie to her. I had in fact been doing research.

~~~~~~~

"Is there anyone here that wishes to speak to me?" I asked, and then nervously glanced around the cemetery. "Is there someone here who asked for prayer? Please tell me your name." *God, I hope no one is watching me,* I remember thinking as I continued with my questions. "Why are you here? Do you need help?" If my questions were being answered I could not hear them.

I suddenly felt very foolish standing there in the middle of the graveyard with my tape recorder, talking to someone or something I couldn't see or hear. "Well I have to be going now, goodbye," I said as I took another glance around. If anyone was watching, I didn't see them. They would have surely doubted my sanity. As I said, I grew up in that church and everyone knows either me or my family.

I was especially thankful I hadn't run into the Pastor. As much as I'd hate to have to lie to him, I would not have dared tell him the truth. *And just what is the truth?* I wondered as I made the short drive home. Maybe the tape recorder held some clues.

Research, by definition, is the diligent and systematic inquiry into a subject to discover or revise facts, theories, etc. according to Webster's American Dictionary. I defined the word in much simpler terms. To me it was simply a quest for knowledge. I hadn't started this new course of study with the notion of revising facts or forming any theories. I just wanted answers—answers to the questions keeping me awake at night. Why did these voices speak to me? What could they possibly want? What could it possibly mean? I wasn't imagining them. They were there on my recorder. But what I recorded on that day brought up more questions. Now I wasn't so sure I really wanted to know the answers.

"Knowledge can be painful," was the only reply I got from my ten minutes of tape at the cemetery. The voice appeared on my
~~~~~~~

recorder just after I asked, *Why are you here? Do you need help?* It was not just a faint whisper this time, as on my initial visit. This was a deep voice, deeper than mine. I could hear the wisdom of the ages in the weathered voice. Was this some sort of warning? And if so, was it meant for me?

I definitely felt like I was somewhere I didn't belong. I almost felt guilty about my being there, in that quiet place of the dead. Aren't some things better left alone? Were there some questions better left unanswered? Is that what the voice was trying to tell me?

A chill ran down my spine. I thought back on the adage *everything happens for a reason*. I sat and pondered these questions for quite some time, trying to make sense of it all. Maybe I shouldn't go back there. But I still had questions! Questions haunting me—consuming me. Maybe I should go back. Maybe just once more I thought... Yet another old saying suddenly came to mind, *curiosity killed the cat.*

~~~~~~~

"For Christ died for sins once for all, the righteous for the unrighteous, to bring you to God. He was put to death in the body, but made alive by the Spirit, through who also he went and preached to the spirits in prison who disobeyed long ago when God waited patiently in the days of Noah while the ark was being built..." (1 Peter 3:18-20). If I heard this scripture before, it fell on the deaf ears of my youth.

But on that day, as I sat on the hard wooden pew in the eleven o'clock service, the Pastor's words captured my full, undivided attention. Why pick that day to read those verses from the book of Peter? Why did I pick this day to attend for the first time since my injury? I hadn't made it to church in almost a year. My back just wouldn't tolerate it.

Spirits in prison were the words that jolted me from my
~~~~~~~

medicated stupor. *Who disobeyed...* Could this have anything to do with my research? A clue to the mystery that so haunted my thoughts lately? And what happened to the *spirits in prison?* The verse does not tell us. However, the Pastor went on to say the interpretations of these verses were many and caused much debate and speculation among the religious leaders of our time. *Everything happens for a reason*, I thought again as I bowed my head for the closing prayer.

CHAPTER THREE

It was a quiet moonless night. A light breeze rustled what leaves were still clinging to the ancient oak tree that stood in the center of the burial ground. I wasn't as worried about my being seen this time. *At least not by the living*. It was almost midnight when I parked around the back of the church, pulling up the drive with the car lights extinguished. I made my way to the entrance gate, only to find it was locked. My back screamed in protest as I stepped over the stone wall into the graveyard. *Knowledge can be painful,* I thought as I grimaced. If I felt uneasy there before, it was nothing in comparison to what I was now feeling. "God, I must be crazy," I muttered as I approached the giant old tree.

This feeling is hard for me to describe, but if skin can crawl then I believe mine did that night. I experienced this feeling once before, on another night long, long ago. In that same place—inside those very walls.

It was a sultry summer evening. I must have been around

seventeen or so at the time. That night would become a memorable one for me. Not only because I experienced my first real kiss earlier in the afternoon before youth meeting, but what I would experience later, just as the sun set on that hot Sabbath day. They say *time clouds the memory* and that may be so as the young girl's face has all but faded from mine. The innocence of youth seems to slip away from us a little at a time. It is replaced by facts, sometimes hard facts–facts about life, about love, about hate... About death. And so it would be for me on that night.

"Run, Steve, run!" I could hear my teammates laughing and cheering as I rounded third base and headed for home. I wasn't running though, I was walking at a rather casual pace. It was the bottom of the ninth inning and I was about to score the winning run. I couldn't take credit for our win. Bryan Furr was the batter who just hit a home run over the cemetery wall. I only got a single when I was at bat. All I had to do was walk around the bases. It was our usual Sunday evening, youth, softball game always followed with homemade ice cream. As I said, it was hot and I was glad to see the sun begin to dip behind the trees. When we were gathering up the bases, bats, and other equipment, we suddenly realized the ball was missing.

"I'll go and get it," I offered. It was still in the graveyard, somewhere. I stepped over the wall and began my search, still wiping sweat from my eyes. "Come on, where is it?" I wondered, as I ventured deeper inside the rows of stone. The shadows were growing long and the place held a surreal feeling. As I wandered through the twilight, I felt as if I were not alone. Then I saw him, lying face down in the grass. Sprawled out between two grave markers, he was dressed in a black suit.

"Hey, Mister, are you okay?" I nervously asked him. "Sir, can I help you?" I inquired, as I squinted to see in the failing light. I slowly approached the prone figure. *Was he asleep? Was he sick? Was someone playing a joke?* I reached down and gently shook him. "Wake up."Getting no response I kneeled down beside him and rolled him over.

He was an elderly gentleman. His eyes were wide open, his mouth agape in what looked to be a silent scream. I fell backward in horror as an insect scurried out. There was earth and grass in his clenched fists as if he had been trying to pull himself up. His dim eyes stared back at me in the gloom. They were lifeless and cold. Now it was I who screamed. I scrambled backward and away from him. Our eyes still locked in that unearthly gaze.

"Call the police, call an ambulance!" I shouted as I bolted into the fellowship hall. "There's a dead man in the graveyard!" I exclaimed as I struggled to find my breath. The room erupted in laughter. "No, I'm not kidding! There is a dead man in the cemetery," I panted.

"Yeah, we know. They're all dead out there, Steve," someone joked as the laughter continued.

"I'm dead serious," I shouted. This statement only brought more laughter from the teens. "It looked like old Mr. Foard," I informed them as I stood there trembling.

The laughter suddenly stopped. Everyone in our church knew Mr. Frank Foard, the kindly old widower who taught Bible school and would never miss a Sunday service. The old gentleman lived beside the cemetery for longer than any of us had been born. The police suspected no foul play when he died.

"Poor old guy probably had a heart attack on his way home from church this morning," was what the cop said as they were loading his stiff body into the coroners van. *Natural causes* was what they wrote in their report. I hadn't seen anything *natural* about it. He surely died a terrible death. I could see it on his face, in that lifeless stare…in his silent scream. Yes, *time clouds the memory.* But sometimes not well enough. I will never forget that night. The first time my skin crawled. I have often wished I could.

~~~~~~~

“Jubel?” Where had I heard that name before? It was there on my recorder just as it had been inscribed on the toppled headstone I filmed just over a week before. Could this be the name of the entity that whispered, *Pray for me*? Or was it Jubel who tried to warn me? *Just more damn questions!* I thought.

I hoped my late night field trip had yielded some answers, but I was not finding this to be the case. It hadn't been a total waste of time. Yes, I recorded a name. Yes, it had been a name on a headstone in the vicinity where I recorded the voice. But, did it actually prove anything? No, it proved nothing, other than whoever or whatever was there still wanted to talk to me. Was it this presence that caused the creepy feeling which crept over me while I was there? Or could it have been the fact I was alone in that graveyard at midnight, talking to the dead?

I hadn't enjoyed it, whatever the cause may have been. I did know I never wanted to feel that sensation again. The voice said something else as well. At least, it sounded like the same voice. It came toward the end of my visit and now had me wondering what meaning it might hold.

"My ship awaits us," the voice whispered into the tape recorder.

"For this cause was the gospel preached also to them that are dead, that they might be judged according to men in the flesh, but live according to God in spirit." (1 Peter 4:6)

This is interesting, I thought as I stared at the scripture. I had not slept well lately and though my mind was weary, it would not rest. *Judged according to men in the flesh.* Meaning God judged them by their deeds on earth. *Live according to God in spirit.* Did
~~~~~~~

this mean the spirits were allowed into heaven? Or did they dwell somewhere *in-between?*

Could any of this have to do with my research? The systematic and diligent inquiry of a subject I could not understand. *Wasn't the purpose of research to find facts?* I asked myself. The fact was I only found more questions. Although the questions seemed to be relevant to the subject matter, I had no answers! Then, another thought unexpectedly came to mind, *Does a madman realize he is insane?* I certainly hoped so.

My late night studies ended with my dozing off. My neck was stiff and my back reminded me I was getting too old to sleep in a chair. The Bible lay closed on my lap, the house dark except for the small lamp I read by. I couldn't have been asleep for more than a couple of hours. I glanced at the clock through bleary eyes. It was three in the morning.

What woke me? I wondered through my daze. Not a stiff neck, nor my aching back. A gentle tugging on my shirt collar had coaxed me from my uneasy rest. Did I imagine this, or had my wife come in to wake me? In either case, I was ready to trade the desk chair for our bed.

"Lynn... Honey?" I called softly as I felt my way into the dark bedroom. She was sound asleep, it couldn't have been her. *Maybe I was dreaming*, I thought as I slipped out of my clothing and in between the bed sheets. But there was no more time to think about it then. I quickly fell into a deep, much needed sleep.

My ship awaits us. Those haunting words sounded to me to be from another time, a different era. What exactly were they trying to say? Were the dead just making idle conversation, or did the words hold some sort of meaning? Had the voice been addressing me... Or informing me? The word *my* implied ownership. *Ship* meaning vessel, a means of transportation. *Awaits* meaning waiting in expectation, and *us* being plural, meant more than one.

"Dear God," I thought aloud. Could I be the ship... *The vessel?* Maybe it wasn't addressing or informing me after all. *Could the voice have been... Referring to me?*

My thoughts were then interrupted by a very cold, wet nose on my elbow. I must have jumped a foot out of my chair. "Damn it, Cruzer! Don't sneak up on me like that!" I swore, my back now hurting from the sudden upward jolt. The lab sat there grinning up at me like he had no clue what I was swearing about. "Are you laughing at me, mutt?" By the look he gave, I couldn't help but think he was. "You're just a phone call away from becoming a pound puppy. You do realize that, don't you, mutt?" I asked him.

His only reply to my scolding was a big yawn. He paid no attention to my idle threats. He knew who was master of this abode. He was! At least as far as he was concerned. I was just there for his convenience. Someone to refill the dog food dispenser and open the back door whenever he asked. Someone to top off the water bowl and scoop his poop. And being such a kind and thoughtful master, he even let me sleep in his bed. *Yes, he must surely love me,* I thought, as he led me down the hallway toward the back door.

Then he suddenly did the strangest thing… He stopped dead in his tracks, his head slowly tilting from one side to the other. He then emitted a long, low growl at whatever it was he saw or heard. He took a couple more steps then halted again. The fur on his back bristled as he gave another deep guttural growl. So there we both stood, staring down the corridor, our senses fully alert. Our ears strained to hear the slightest sound, our eyes straining to see something... *Something unseen?*

"What is it, boy?" I whispered as the dog crouched in the hallway, his eyes still fixed on nothing. He then let out a half–hearted, little bark as if not quite sure what he was barking at.

Eventually, he stood up and proceeded into the den then curled up in his favorite chair, as if nothing strange ever happened.

Great! I remember thinking. *My dog's gone crazy, too!*

CHAPTER FOUR

Curiosity killed the cat, I reflected as I stepped through the iron gateway. I had reservations about returning to the cemetery, but it seemed inevitable. My research demanded it! I decided to bring the camcorder along this time. It would add an additional source of audio, as well as visual documentation. I didn't plan to film more headstones, however.

I set the camera down on the fallen stone of the Pharr brothers' grave and left it filming as I meandered nearby with my tape recorder. I hoped to hear more from Jubel. Perhaps he would speak into the camera, or maybe it would record them talking amongst themselves. I didn't know if all of this would produce any evidence, but I couldn't record them without returning—without trying.

"At least, it isn't dark this time." I shuddered as I thought back on my previous visit and the uneasy feeling that crept over me then. No, I would never go back there after dark, I was sure of that. If the dead had anything more to say to me they would have to say it by the light of day.

An orb, by definition, is a ball or sphere. Could that explain what I was seeing on my new film footage? *Some researchers believe these orbs to be the manifestation of spirit energy*, the article read. I wasn't certain I agreed with that theory, but I was certain something unusual had been captured on my camera that day. It appeared to be round and made of light, or maybe some kind of mist. It was about the size of a dinner plate and gray in color. It was a miracle I filmed it at all, whatever it was.

As I prepared to exit the cemetery, I knelt down in front of the camera to turn it off. I noticed my shoe was untied, so while I knelt, I took the opportunity to re-tie it. It was then the *orb* or mist appeared. It swooped down from above, partially covering my face as it continued slowly downward along my chest. It proceeded to glide down my leg until it reached the ground, where it just disappeared. Five seconds later and I would have turned off my camera. I wouldn't even have noticed it if I hadn't worn dark clothing that day, but it was faintly visible against the darker background.

Just another mystery to ponder, I thought. Then there was the voice. It hadn't appeared on my camera audio, but only on my tape recorder. My research that day resulted in what I hoped could be a tangible clue. It sounded to me like the same whispering voice I recorded on my earlier visits. But this time it was louder, clearer.

It spoke two separate sentences, one behind the other. "You must help us! We're not dead!"

For this cause the gospel was preached also to the dead. I reflected back on the book of Peter. *But live according to God in spirit.* This verse kept me up late again. Could this hold any relevance to what the voice at the cemetery stated? If they are not dead as the voice proclaimed then were they in spirit? And if they were in spirit, then how was I to help them? I wondered. Are they somehow attached to their earthly remains? I pondered. If not, why were they hanging out in the graveyard?

“You must help us!”

“We're not dead!”

I played the recording again. How many spirits were there?

These questions played over and over in my tired mind and I couldn't help but entertain an earlier thought. *Does a madman question his own sanity? Does he realize he is insane?* Would I have to be crazy to continue this course of study, the systematic research of a subject I could not comprehend? *No, I wouldn't have to be, I reasoned, but it just might help*, I concluded. I still hadn't mentioned any of this to Lynn. She was on a need to know basis, I decided. And right now she didn't need to know.

And what would I tell her anyway? I wondered. That her husband had been spending his mornings standing alone in a graveyard talking to the dead? And they were answering? *Nope, I couldn't tell her that.* She would surely think I had lost my mind. My thoughts were soon interrupted by another faint tug. This time I wasn't asleep so I knew I hadn’t dreamed it and I didn't think I could have imagined it. I quickly spun in my chair, only to find no one there. "God, I must be losing it!" I said out loud. I switched off the lamp and retired to bed for the evening.

~~~~~~~

"Steve," my wife softy whispered my name.

"Huh... What?" I muttered as I struggled to shake the cobwebs of sleep from my mind. "Yes, honey?" I answered again. I rolled onto my side and placed my arms around her, but she wasn't there.

Cruzer lay beside me in her place, growling in protest as I gave him the hug intended for her. It wasn't a warning, but more of a complaint. "Can't you see I’m trying to sleep? How dare you
~~~~~~~

disturb me this early?" He asked me in his disgruntled growl. After all, it was his bed! At least, as far as he was concerned.

“Lynn... Honey?” I called out to her. No answer. I glanced at the alarm clock to see it was well after ten a.m. I threw off the covers and slowly climbed out of bed. “Lynn?" I called again, as I stumbled down the hallway into the den. Then I realized it could not have been my wife who spoke my name. She had to be at work by nine and the car was gone from the driveway.

So... Who or *what* whispered into my ear? I wondered in my confusion. Could I have been dreaming? If I had in fact, heard a soft voice whisper my name, what could it mean? Straight jackets and padded walls? Obviously Cruzer didn't hear it, or if he did he didn't react. "It must have been a dream," I reasoned. I certainly hoped it was. *Does a madman realize he is insane?* I certainly hoped not. There would be no more time to think about that then. I was going back to the graveyard.

~~~~~~~

"Are you trapped here?" I paused for several seconds to give the voices ample time to respond. "Why do you linger in this place?" I waited. "How can I help you?" My questions to the dead were abruptly interrupted by one from the living.

"What ya doin', friend?"

I must have jumped a foot off the ground. I glanced around to see Mr. Bowers, the church custodian, standing right behind me. He gave me quite a start, as I didn't realize he was there until he spoke.

"Just some research," I answered, wondering how long he had been standing there.

"Sorry if I scared ya" he said, as he spat a brown stream of tobacco juice.

For some reason, I didn‘t quite believe him.

"Didn't I see you here yesterday?" he asked.
~~~~~~~

"Why yes, I did stop by the cemetery for a few minutes yesterday morning," I replied as I wondered what he was leading up too.

"I think I know what you're doing," he informed me.

Oh crap! Did he know about my research? Had he overheard me?

"You're one of them... One of them... Oh, what do ya call em'?"

"Genealogist?" I offered.

"Yeah, that's it!" he exclaimed. "A genealogist, that's what you are," he said, as if he were the one who enlightened me.

I let out a sigh of relief. *If he only knew*, I thought.

"Do you have relatives buried here?" he inquired.

"No" I replied. "Just a few friends." I could tell my statement confused him somewhat by the puzzled look on his face as he glanced down at the tombstones in front of me. They were over a hundred and fifty years old. With that I bid him good day. "Let him chew on that." I chuckled to myself as I headed home.

"Why do you linger in this place?" I reviewed my short recording, but doubted it would produce any results. I hadn't been at the cemetery five minutes before the custodian unknowingly botched my field trip. I grinned as I thought back on the look he gave me. Had he thought I was nuts? I couldn't help but think he had. I was leaning toward that theory myself.

"Are you trapped here?" The tape played on yielding no replies. "Come on!" I mumbled out loud. "Answer me, damn it!" The recording was nearing its end. Then, just before I asked how I could help them, I heard a voice not my own. And no, it wasn't Mr. Bower's. What this voice had to tell me was very clear. Could it have something to do with my research? The diligent and systematic inquiry into my own sanity. I couldn't help but think it just might.

“Steve…” There was that voice again. But this time, to my relief, it was in fact, my wife.

“Yes, dear,” I answered.

“Can we talk about something for a moment?” She asked.

I had no idea what this conversation might be about, but her tone suggested she had something serious on her mind.

“Sure,” I answered as I wondered where this was leading.

“If I were to tell you something, whatever it might be… Would you believe me?” Her look suggested she was somehow uncertain what my answer might be.

“Of course I would, my dear,” I assured her. I had no reason not to. After all, we’d been married for almost thirty years and I could easily tell if she was lying about something. Not that she would ever lie to me, I’m not implying that, but if she did I would certainly know. Thirty years is quite a long time to get to know someone.

“I’ve been hearing things lately,” she hesitantly confided.

“What kind of things?” I urged her on.

“Strange things... Things I can’t explain,” she whispered as if she feared our conversation might somehow be overheard. “At first I thought I was imagining them,” she slowly continued.

“What do they sound like?” I asked, leaning closer in order to hear. The expression on her face told me she was not looking forward to what she would tell me next.

“Voices,” she whispered. “I hear voices!”

Knowledge can be painful, flashed through my mind as I stared into those distraught blue eyes. “Tell me more,” I coaxed her, not really sure if I wanted to hear anymore.

“Sometimes they are just whispers,” she went on in that haunted tone. “Sometimes they sound like faint conversations in another room,” she explained. “I can hear them talking, but I can’t make out what's being said. When I go to look, there is no one there." She looked so confused. "Sometimes… They whisper my name!" I could see the terror in her expression. "What do they want?"

"I don't know," I answered.

"Why are they here?"

"I don't know," I repeated.

"Does all of this sound crazy?" she asked me, her voice trembling.

"Yes…" I answered. "That does sound rather crazy… But I hear them too." Now it would be my turn to confess.

~~~~~~~

I rewound the tape and listened again to the words. "Finally!" I exclaimed. A direct answer to my questions, at least to me it sounded like a relevant response. Was my research finally producing some answers? I reflected back on my previous recordings, as I shuffled through my desk drawer for a pen and my notepad. I scribbled the phrases down, one by one. They lay before me like pieces of a bizarre puzzle.

Pray for me, the words that began this quest, must hold some meaning. The phrase, *knowledge can be painful,* certainly seemed to hold some truth thus far, but had not been a direct reply to a question. *My ship awaits us*, although it may fit somewhere, could not be considered a reply so I crossed it out as well. "Good Lord," I whispered as I stared down at the remaining pieces. Answers! My research was yielding answers, I concluded, as I read them in the order they had been spoken. Could this have something to do with the book of Peter? I had no proof, but the evidence almost seemed to fit.

Pray for me… You must help us… We're not dead… We cursed at God!
~~~~~~~

CHAPTER FIVE

"Is the Pastor in?" I inquired. "No sir, he won't be back in his office until Friday," his secretary informed me. "Would you like to leave a message for him?" she politely asked.

"No thanks, I'll come back next week," I replied.

"The Associate Pastor is here, sir. Would you care to speak with him?" she offered as I was turning to leave.

I heard about our new youth pastor who recently joined the church staff, but I had not yet met him. "Sure," I replied, "if he's not too busy." I needed to talk to someone about all this. I wanted some theological insight into what my research had so far uncovered.

I wasn't sure how I should start our conversation or how my visit might be received. *How much should I tell him?* I wondered as he introduced himself and asked me to have a seat.

"What's on your mind, Mr. Hill? How can I help you?" he warmly inquired. He was a young man, much younger than I expected. He couldn't be more than thirty or so.

"I'm not sure where I should start," I said as I wondered if he could fathom what was on *my* mind.

"Why don't you start at the beginning," he suggested.

And so he sat there patiently as I told him everything. How I accidentally recorded the whisper asking for prayer. How I returned to the graveyard trying to record more phantom voices in an effort to find answers to questions I could not even comprehend. About the haunting correlation between my research and the book of Peter. How we had been hearing the whispering voices at home. How oddly my dog was behaving of late. How I even doubted my own sanity.

"Does a madman question his own sanity, Pastor?" I asked as I finished relaying my ludicrous sounding story.

No reply. I sat there studying the expression on his face. He would choose his words carefully, is what it said.

"Just because I don't know how to respond to you, does not mean I think you are crazy," he finally answered. "I do believe you think you hear these things and they are affecting you in an adverse way," he went on to explain. "The teachings of our faith tell us there is only one ghost—the Holy Ghost."

"But what about the *spirits in prison*?" I interrupted. "The ones Christ preached to after his resurrection?" I questioned.

"That scripture refers back to the time of Noah, before the great flood," he calmly explained. "That was before the birth of Christ so God chose to imprison the spirits of those who perished in the flood and had not heard the gospel, instead of casting them into hell," he expounded.

"So there is an *in-between*?" I again interrupted. "What if this *prison* the scripture refers to still exists today? A place filled with restless souls who are either lost or trapped in some unseen realm.

Souls not pure enough to enter heaven, but not so unrighteous as to be cast into the pit. Maybe the scripture applies to modern times as well as the time of Noah," I suggested.

His reply was a thoughtful silence.

"For this cause was the gospel preached also to them that are dead, that they might be judged according to men in the flesh, but live according to God in spirit."

His eyebrows rose at my quoting of the scripture. "The teachings of our doctrine make no mention of such a place. Therefore, I do not believe it exists," was his careful reply.

"Okay, Pastor, then explain the voices," I challenged. "Do you think I am just making all this up?"

"I don't know what to think," was his answer. "I do believe you think you hear them," he repeated, as if that would somehow explain them.

What I heard from his statements was, *I think you must be crazy!* "Here, listen for yourself," I said as I reached into my coat pocket for my tape recorder.

"Wow," he exclaimed as he suddenly glanced at his watch. "It's getting late and I need to pick up my son from daycare. It's been a pleasure talking with you, Mr. Hill," he said as he stood and opened the door for me. "I hate to cut this short, but I really must be going."

"Sure," I replied and thanked him for his time.

No, that didn't go so well, I thought as I climbed into my truck and headed for home. The preacher thought I was mad. I could see it on his face and hear it in those carefully chosen words. Hell, maybe I was crazy. I obviously convinced him by the way he rushed to be rid of me. One thing I did realize was I would no longer be attending that church. Not after our conversation. Nope, that hadn't gone too well at all. I had not intended to tell him everything. Not after I exercised so much caution to keep my research covert. But it felt so good to talk about it, to get it off my chest. Even though the young Pastor now thought me insane, it still felt very, very good. *Everything happens for a reason.*

~~~~~~~

'Shadow people,' according to Wikipedia, an online encyclopedia, 'are supernatural, shadow-like beings of both modern folklore and paranormal popular culture that are said to appear as dark forms seen mostly in peripheral vision. Anecdotal reports of shadow people occupy a similar role in popular culture to ghost sightings.'

Could this be what my wife encountered last evening? It seemed to match what she described to me. She had been curled up in bed next to Cruzer and I reading a magazine when she glanced up to see the dark silhouette outlined on our open bedroom door. She said it was there for only a couple of seconds and then it just vanished.

"Why didn't you tell me about this last night?" I scolded her.

"You were already snoring, and exactly what was I to tell you, dear?" she asked. "Quick, wake up… Look at what is no longer there. Besides, I thought maybe I was just…seeing things."

"What did it look like?" I inquired.

"Just a shadow," she answered.

"What did it appear to be doing?" I prodded, trying to get her to describe the sighting in more detail."

"He was just standing there… Watching," she said.

"So what did you do after you saw…or thought you saw… him?" I asked her.

"I turned out the lamp and went to sleep. I have to work, remember?" She yawned as she reluctantly climbed from between the bed sheets.
~~~~~~~

"Heard any more voices?" I asked, hoping her answer would be no.

"Not in the last couple of days," she replied. "There is one thing, though, that has been bothering me, Stephen."

"What now?" I thought out loud.

"I guess I could have imagined it."

"What?" I insisted.

"Oh, it's probably nothing," she said.

"Imagined what?" I asked her again. Cruzer growled in protest as I kicked off the covers and followed her down the hallway into the kitchen.

"Oh, it was probably nothing" she repeated.

"Tell me, Lynn!" I implored her.

"It's probably nothing... But a couple of times the other evening while I sat reading, I thought I felt something...tugging on my shirt."

My ship awaits us! I reflected. Judging from the strange occurrences we both experienced, I now felt my original theory must hold some merit. After all, I had been there in the graveyard, waiting in expectation. *Had I, in fact, been the ship—the vessel? Had they simply climbed aboard, sailed right out of the cemetery, and into my living room?* Castaways from another time...another realm? It seemed my theory might now be a haunting fact. I had not yet mentioned the faint tugs I, myself, felt so I doubted Lynn imagined them. *What in the hell have I brought into this house?* I wondered.

"I don't know, Stephen," she replied. "What have you brought into our house?"

~~~~~~~

Metroareaparanormalsociety.com. 'We ain't scared!' That's what the website boldly stated. I stared at the phone number listed
~~~~~~~

on the home page. Call for a free, confidential investigation. The number was local so I decided to dial it and see who might answer.

"MAPS, Joe speaking," the voice on the other end informed me.

"Hi Joe, this is Steve. I got your number from your website and wanted to ask you a few questions."

"Sure," he replied.

"If I told you I was experiencing unexplained activity in my home, would you be interested in helping me?" I inquired.

"What kind of activity? he asked.

I detected a note of excitement in his voice. "Oh, let's see... Whispering voices, shadow men, our clothing being pulled by some unseen force, and my dog acting weird. That's about it," I told him, as I wondered if it sounded as crazy to him as it did to me.

"When would you like us there, sir?" he asked, in an even more excited tone. "How about this afternoon?" he suggested.

"Sure, I'll be home all day," I answered.

"We'll see you around five for a preliminary investigation and interview," he assured me.

I emailed him my street address and anxiously awaited their arrival. I was hoping they could give me some answers as to what Lynn and I experienced. I decided not to tell them about my research as I didn't want to influence their investigation. I knew where the entities came from. I just hoped MAPS could tell me why they were here, what they might want, and how to get rid of them.

Cruzer let out a bark as they pulled into the drive.

"Quiet, mutt!" I instructed as I opened the door to greet them. "I'm Joe and this is Tina, our founder. Tina is our team sensitive. If there is anything paranormal going on here, she will feel it," he confidently informed me. "Do you mind if we record the client interview?" he asked.

Client? For some reason the word reminded me of the old black and white Perry Mason episodes I watched as a kid. *My client has no objections, your honor.* "No, I have no objections," I told him. "You may proceed."

We seated ourselves in the den and I proceeded to relate to them what he referred to as my *claims of activity.* When I finished, he proceeded to ask me a series of interview questions they assured me were routine. I felt like I was on trial, though, the recorder serving as a digital stenographer.

"Have you or anyone in your family ever been diagnosed with a mental illness?"

No, not yet. "No, not that I'm aware of," I answered.

"Did you attend college?" he inquired.

"No," I answered.

"Are you, or have you, ever been addicted to drugs or alcohol?"

"No!" My doctor advised me not to drink alcohol as it would hinder my recovery. The only drugs I had taken had been prescribed.

"Have you or anyone who lives here ever experimented with or used an Ouija board?"

"Hell no!" I told him. "I'm not into séances." I was into research.

"Have you ever questioned your own mental status?" was his next question.

Objection, your Honor! Objection overruled, just answer the question! "Does a madman question his own sanity?" I sidestepped his question with one of my own. Perry would have been proud.

"I wouldn't know," he finally answered.

"Next question," I said.

"Do you mind if we look around?" He then asked rather timidly as he laid his questionnaire aside.

No further questions. The defense rests. "Nope," I replied. "Go right ahead."

MAPS then proceeded to slowly tour my humble abode with an Electromagnetic Field Meter, or EMF detector, as they called it. Joe explained that some paranormal researchers believe the device can detect the presence of spirits.

"The theory is that ghosts are made up of energy," he explained. "This meter measures fluctuations in the electromagnetic field. If they are here, this unit will detect them," he enlightened me. "Tina is using a digital thermometer which we use to measure temperature changes."

No shit, Sherlock! I thought.

"Some researchers believe that when a ghost is present it utilizes the energy in the environment to manifest itself. This drawing of energy creates hot or cold spots we can measure and document with this device," he patiently said.

"What's Tina doing now…praying?" I asked him.

She stood in the middle of my bedroom with her head bowed and her arms extended, her palms turned upward.

"She is using her psychic abilities to attempt to contact the entity," he informed me in a whisper. "Do you know what EVP stands for?" he then asked.

"Yes, Electronic Voice Phenomena," I answered.

He looked rather shocked that I would know this.

"I read an article about it one time," I told him.

"Great," he said. "When we get through with our EMF and temperature sweeps, we'd like to conduct an EVP session here."

"I have no objections," I said. "You may proceed."

"Is there anyone here who would like to speak to us?" He paused. "Can you give us a sign of your presence? If you can hear me, can you make a noise?"

Our ears strained to hear the slightest sound.

"Can you knock three times on the wall?"

Nothing.

"Could you tug on my shirt?"

We waited.

"Tell us your name!" he demanded. "Well, I think we're finished here for now," he said as he switched off the recorder.

"Do you think we got anything?" I anxiously inquired as they were heading towards the front door.

"We'll be in touch" he replied.

"When would you like to schedule the full investigation?" I asked him.

"We'll be in touch," he repeated as they scurried down the sidewalk.

What he might as well have said was, *don't call us, we'll call you.* At least that's what I heard in those words he so hastily spoke. They had been there for only thirty minutes in all. At first they acted like they couldn't wait to get here. Now they acted like they couldn't leave fast enough. *What scared them off,* I wondered. *Me*... I concluded.

~~~~~~~

"You don't look so good," Doctor Ash stated.

"I haven't been sleeping so well lately," I confessed.

"Has the pain been causing you to lose sleep?" he inquired. He could probably see the bags under my eyes. "Your latest MRI results indicate you suffered some nerve damage resulting from scar tissue. That could explain the pain down your leg and the numbness in your foot you've been experiencing," he informed me. "I am going to continue your physical therapy visits and prescribe you something to help you sleep."

"You're the doctor," I replied.
~~~~~~~

"I want to see you again in two weeks. How are your other medications holding out?" he asked. "Do you need to refill them?"

"Probably so," I answered.

"I'll write you a refill for them. My nurse will be back with you in a few minutes. You can go ahead and get dressed," he finished.

Yes, the pain had cost me some sleep, that had been true enough, I thought as I waited for the nurse to return. But I couldn't tell him about the other causes of my restless nights. Things an MRI couldn't explain—the voices, the shadows. *Nope, I couldn't tell him about my research.*

~~~~~~~

"MAPS, Joe speaking."

"Hi Joe, this is Steve." I informed him.

"Oh… Hi," he responded.

I could tell by his tone he wasn't as excited to hear from me as he was on my initial call. "Joe, it's been over a week since your preliminary investigation and I was just wondering if you had any news for me". I inquired.

"Well… No," he replied. "We found nothing at all."

"When can we schedule the full investigation?" I wanted to know.

"I'll have to get back to you on that," he said.

"Okay, no problem, just let me know."

He ended our conversation with a promise to get back to me soon. The fact that their initial investigation hadn't produced any evidence did not particularly surprise me. After all, it took me at least four visits to the cemetery to record the evidence I did have. The thing that did surprise me, though, was the email I received later that evening.
~~~~~~~

'Dear Mr. Hill,

After careful review of your case, we did not find any evidence of paranormal activity that would substantiate your claims. We would like to thank you for allowing us into your home. If we can ever assist you in the future, please let us know. Sincerely,

Joe Blow, MAPS.'

My client pleads not guilty due to insanity. Case dismissed! That's what I read in that email. *Well, that was short and sweet.* Just like their investigation had been. Nope, no phantom shadows, whispering voices, or shirt tugging entities manifested during their visit. The sensitive hadn't sensed anything and the EMF meter had not fluctuated. There had been no knocking on the wall and all of his EVP questions had gone unanswered. *Too bad the ghost hadn't shown,* I thought. Tina could have taken its temperature.

The sleeping pills seemed to be helping somewhat. At least I was getting more rest. We hadn't experienced any more haunting activity since MAPS had been here. I was beginning to think the spirits had left us. At least, I hoped so. Maybe they just got bored hanging around the house. Lord knows, I certainly was. *Perhaps they followed Joe home,* I giggled to myself.

Were they now over at his place, knocking on walls, and yanking on his shirt? Scaring the shit out of his wife? I didn't know, but I certainly hoped so. Then he could investigate his own haunting. I grinned at the thought of him sitting there answering his own routine questions. The tape recorder bearing silent witness as he questioned himself in regards to his own mental status. *Misery loves company*, I thought. *No... I would not wish that on him.*

I may have been bitter, but I'm not a spiteful person. Besides, I had been the one who called and invited them over. I felt they had been genuine enough in their efforts to help me. I just couldn't figure out exactly why they scurried out of here and didn't plan to return. The email didn't say. Perhaps it had been the question I posed to him. "Does a madman realize he is insane?"

~~~~~~~

"Steve!" There was that voice again.

"He's here!" my wife whispered in my ear as she tried to shake me awake.

"Who's here honey?" I mumbled, as I struggled to emerge from my pill-induced slumber.

"The man!" she excitedly whispered.

"What man?" I asked her, still not completely coherent.

"The shadow man," she answered.

"Where?" I muttered, slowly starting to emerge from the fog.

"He was right there," she whispered. "Standing in the doorway…watching."

"Cruzer saw him too," she said.

"What did he do?" I prodded.

"He growled," she answered.

"The shadow?" I asked her.

"No, Cruzer," she replied.

"What did the *man* do, Lynn?" I wanted all the details. This definitely could have something to do with my research. "Did he just disappear?"

"No… Not this time. He stood there for a few seconds just staring at me then he slowly turned and walked down the hall," she stated. "I could see him block the night light as he walked past."

"I wonder what he wants?" I sighed, my thoughts still clouded by the pills.

"I think he wanted me to follow him."
~~~~~~~

A shiver ran down my surgically altered spine as I pondered what meaning this might hold. Why was he here? Was he, in fact, trying to lure my wife from our bed? And for what purpose? I threw off the sheets and grabbed the flashlight I keep stashed in my nightstand drawer. "Stay here," I told her.

I cautiously crept down the corridor, my senses not fully alert, but my ears straining to hear the slightest sound.

Thump…

What was that? I stopped dead in my tracks. Had I heard something?

Thump…

There it was again! Sounded like it came from… Nowhere?

Thump…

What the hell? Three faint knocks? I thought back to the MAPS investigation. I stood there listening, frozen in time. Tick...tock...tick...tock... I slowly made my way to the end of the corridor. Tick…tock…tick…tock… The mantle clock in the den made the only sound. Tick…tock…tick…tock… I felt like I wasn't alone. Tick…tock…tick…tock… I sensed a dark presence behind me. Tick…

"DAMN IT, CRUZER!" I swore. He snuck up on me again and placed his cold, wet nose on the cheek of my bare behind. His eyes reflected in the beam of the flashlight, his white teeth visible in a mischievous grin. He looked like something out of a 'B-rated' horror movie. *Devil Dog, the Mutt from Hell!*

We proceeded to patrol the remainder of the house, only to find nothing out of place, no one was there. Had the three thumps I heard been in reply to Joe's question? *If you can hear us, give us a sign? Knock three times on the wall, he had asked.* Was the shadow man trying to tell me something? I wasn't sure, but I couldn't help but think he just might be.

CHAPTER SIX

My research, in fact, resulted in evidence. Evidence that some of us don't necessarily go either up or down when we depart this life. Yes, it proved, at least I considered it proof, that there is a form of afterlife that doesn't involve pearly gates or fiery depths. Perhaps a dark place, a place of shadows—a place somewhere *in-between.*

Our uninvited house guests had been a haunting side effect of my studies, I concluded. I still had many questions indeed. The Pastor talked about angels and Satan. *Everlasting life or eternal damnation. Your choice, choose wisely!* MAPS, who apparently believed in the existence of ghosts, obviously didn't believe me either. So what was I dealing with here? I didn't think the shadow man was an angel, he had no wings. Not according to my wife's description. What purpose could he hope to achieve? I needed more clues. I had no one else to turn to for the answers. I would have to find them for myself, I surmised. If my research brought him here, then perhaps research could yield more answers as to why. Or would it just result in more unanswered questions?

Yes, *knowledge can be painful* and maybe curiosity indeed killed the cat, but I could not find answers without recording them—without trying. I would conduct my own investigation. This house would be my hunting ground, the shadow man my quarry. I would continue where Joe left off. I would become my own client. After all, I already filled out the questionnaire.

Tick…tock…tick…tock… The mantle clock marked the passing of the night. I set my new camera up in the den, aiming it down the hallway towards our bedroom. I adjusted the amount of light in the dim corridor until I determined it was just right. I left open the doors to the guest bedroom, the hall bath, and my office. A faint glow shown from each room and I left the night light plugged into the outlet in the hallway. The trap was set!

If the shadow man chose to show himself tonight, I would know it. Any dark forms that crept down the hallway would be caught on film. Any phantom voices or knocks would be captured on the audio. The camera doesn't blink! At least, that is, until it runs out of film. I hit the record button and retired to the bedroom. The camera would bear silent witness, at least for an hour, until the tape ran out.

He had shown himself to Lynn around midnight last evening, so eleven thirty was the time I thought my vigil should begin. I planned to rise each hour and change my cassettes. I could sleep tomorrow… Tonight I was wide awake! The house was unusually quiet and I laid there, watching for the slightest shadow, listening for the slightest noise that might signal his presence. Tick…tock… tick…tock… The mantle clock in the den was the only sound.

~~~~~~~

"Steve… Are you awake?"

"I am now," I groggily replied.
~~~~~~~

"Don't be late for your physical therapy," my wife said as she rushed to get dressed for work.

"Crap!" I forgot about it again. There certainly had been a lot on my mind lately. I apparently forgot not to fall asleep as well. "Damn it!" I swore. I hadn't stayed up and changed the tapes. *Well, at least I will have an hour's worth of film to review.* I should have never gotten into bed, but I wanted him to think I was fast asleep. Just as I had been the two previous times he had shown himself. I freed myself from my linens and climbed into the shower. I wasn't looking forward to my therapy, but at least it would get my mind out of the house and back to the living.

I checked the camera on the way out, only to find it had been paused. The display window stated it had forty five minutes of tape remaining. *That's rather odd,* I thought. I knew for a fact I left it recording when I went to bed. But there wasn't time to think about that now. I was running late for my therapy appointment. I thought I'd stop by the camera shop on the way home and ask an expert. Perhaps the factory trained technician there could explain the camera's odd behavior.

~~~~~~~

"May I help you?" the tech asked.

"Yes, I bought a camcorder from you a few weeks ago and I have a technical question."

"Oh yes, Mr. Hill, I remember you. You purchased the 250R. What's your question?" he politely asked.

"What could cause the camera to go to pause when it is in the record mode?" I inquired.

"Well... I can think of only two possible reasons," he said. "The first being you accidentally hit the record button twice, which would pause the recording."

"And the second?" I asked.
~~~~~~~

“That the camera ran out of film,” he stated.

“Oh…okay, thanks,” I said as I turned to leave. “Did I hit the record button twice?” I questioned myself. Nope, I didn’t think so. I could remember seeing the red *recording* indicator as I looked back down the hallway last night and the camera had plenty of film left when I checked it this morning. So… If I hadn’t inadvertently dumb thumbed it, and it wasn’t out of film, what could have caused it? Someone else hit pause was the only explanation I could come up with.

Tick…tock…tick…tock… The mantle clock was the only sound on the audio, other than the faint whirling of the cassette drive. Tick…tock…tick…tock… I watched myself walk to the end of the hallway then glance back at the camera as I turned and entered the bedroom. Tick…tock…tick…tock… At twelve minutes into the tape I heard faint snoring. Tick…tock…tick…tock… My footage produced no lurking shadows. Tick…tock…tick…tock… At fourteen-thirty-five on the film, I heard myself snore a little louder. Tick…tock…tick…tock… At fourteen-fifty-three the camera suddenly lost focus. Tick…tock… The tape neared its end. Tick…tock…tick…tock…

”OFF!” Tick… And then nothing.

“What the hell?” I wondered out loud. I quickly rewound the film and listened to the voice again.

“OFF!” Had the shadow man known I was trying to film him? Yes, I reasoned, he must have. He was apparently smarter than I thought. A chill came over me as another thought entered my mind. Had he been watching me set up the camera? Had he figured out how to operate it by watching me turn it on and hit the record button? It certainly seemed so. Damn… How smart was this thing? *Smarter than I, apparently*. If I was to prove he existed, I would have to be more covert in my efforts. *What have I brought into this house?* I wondered again.

~~~~~~~

Having been raised on a farm, I happen to know a thing or two about hunting. I spent many of the days of my youth wandering the creek banks, tracking the different woodland critters that reside there. I eventually became rather proficient at identifying the various tracks. Raccoon, opossum, rabbits, deer, and the elusive bobcat were my boyhood prey.

The critter I now pursued left no tracks, only shadows. He was craftier than any coon, more elusive than any bobcat… Smarter than any fox. I was out to shoot him, but with my camera, not my gun. Not for sport, but for my research. I would need to form a new plan if I was to capture him as evidence. Yes, I would have to outfox him!

I drove down to the electronics store and picked up a new toy. A digital recorder that featured an adjustable voice activation mode. My old tape recorder could only record for thirty minutes until it ran out of tape—the camera only for an hour. With the voice activation, the new recorder could rest in standby mode, recording only if activated by a voice or sound. It could record all night without my having do a thing.

I spent the rest of the afternoon experimenting with my camcorder. I wanted to see if I could explain why it jumped out of focus for a few seconds before it had been paused. There was nothing visible on the film to explain it. Something had to cause its odd behavior, I reasoned. Yes… *Something unseen,* I concluded.

~~~~~~~

"Are you coming to bed?" my wife asked.

"Yes, dear," I said as I switched off my reading lamp. I casually slipped the digital recorder out of my desk drawer doing my best to conceal it from anything that might be watching. Pushing record, as

I crossed the dark hallway, I placed it on the bookshelf at the end of the corridor. I then entered the bedroom and closed the door, hoping my actions had gone unnoticed. While at the electronics store, I also purchased a roll of black electrical tape. I used a small piece to cover the red indicator light on the recorder. The trap was set! As I lay in bed waiting to drift off, I was reminded of another time I tried to outfox a fox.

On a cold winter afternoon, I stood motionless at the edge of the thicket, my ears straining to hear the slightest sound. I was confident I would get them that day. I found their tracks where they crossed the creek and then followed them through the sandy soil of the creek bottom. If I could only find their den, I would have them. The shadows were growing long and it would soon be too dark to see. So I decided to wait at the edge of the field.

Our chickens had been disappearing lately and I had been after the culprits for days. I was probably around fifteen or so at the time and hurried home from school each day to trade my books for my shotgun. Then I briefly glimpsed them as they bounded back into the woods. "Damn it!" I swore out loud.

They had been heading right for me then turned and disappeared back into the shadows, like phantoms. Two gray foxes had been my quarry that day and I was disappointed to not have seen them in time to get off a shot. What gave me away? I wondered. They smelled me, I concluded. Now they knew I was hunting them. I would have to be crafty…crafty indeed!

The next morning I found the new recorder definitely captured something. It showed five separate activations on the display screen. I couldn't wait to listen to what the dead might have to say, if anything, when they thought I couldn't hear. I slid the recorder off the bookcase and into my pocket then proceeded down the hallway and out the front door. I climbed into my truck and headed down to the coffee house. I purchased a large, black cup of joe and sat in my truck looking at the recorder.

Something certainly activated it. Probably my snoring, I chuckled to myself. Yep, I was right. The first two short sound bites were just that, my snores. The third had been a recording of me coughing in my sleep. The fourth caused me to choke on my coffee.

"Smoker's cough," it said. A deep voice, it didn't sound very nice at all. What it had said seemed to be in response to my coughing fit.

"Holy shit!" I exclaimed as the hot coffee sloshed out of the cup and into my lap. The voice spoke just a couple of seconds after my hacking spell. He had been correct! It was a smoker's cough. I quit several years ago but started back recently. My doctor would be furious if he knew about my recovery hindering habit, but I found them to bring me much comfort—something to occupy my hands, something to do during the long hours of my recovery. Another diversion, so to speak, albeit an unhealthy one. If you've never had the habit, you wouldn't understand.

The last activation on my new recorder was a female voice that caused me to ponder new questions. She came in very clear and it sounded as if she were only a few feet from the recorder. "Andy, I love you," she proclaimed.

Andy? I thought. *Who could that be?* And who was the young lady confessing her love for him? For that matter, just what the hell were they doing in my hallway at three thirty in the morning? I didn't know, but I intended to find out. The voices confirmed one thing, though. I was now certain there was more than one.

~~~~~~~

How do you outfox a fox? By deception! I knew the answer from experience. If I let them think they were outsmarting me, then maybe I could trick them into showing themselves. I devised a new
~~~~~~~

plan. After Lynn retired that evening, just after ten o'clock, I set up the camera on its tripod and placed it in the den, just like the previous night I tried to film them. I then adjusted the lighting in the hallway until I figured it was perfect. I turned the camera on then hit the record button, twice, leaving the camera on pause. I proceeded down the corridor and into my office closing the door.

Earlier, I covered the recording indicator light on the camera with black tape. I sat in my office, watching television until just before midnight. I turned out my reading lamp and slipped the camcorder remote control from my desk drawer and into my pants pocket. I then walked down the hallway into the kitchen and got a drink of water. As I passed back through the den I hit the record button on the remote. The faint "beep" confirmed the camera was now recording. I proceeded back down the corridor and retired for the night. The trap was set!

"I heard a shot, did you get him?" my father inquired.

"Yep, I got them," I answered.

"Got them? I only heard one shot," he further questioned me.

"Yes sir, I got them," I repeated, still panting from the long hike home, as I held up two gray fox tails.

"How did you kill two foxes with one shot?" he prodded as if he couldn't quite believe his eyes.

"Lucky shot, I guess," I replied. I talked the school bus driver into stopping by the community store on the way home that afternoon, just long enough for me to run in and purchase the small bottle of female fox urine I ordered a week before.

You don't often see stores like that one anymore. Old country stores that didn't have much of anything, but rather a little of just about everything. From gasoline to Vaseline and anything in between, they had it. If they didn't have what you needed, you could always order it from the catalogue. That's how it was back then, in the days of my youth... Before the days of shopping malls, online showrooms, and same day shipping.

I thought I fooled them into thinking the camera was off, when actually it had been recording from midnight until one am. Then the film expired. I freed the camera from the tripod and proceeded into my office. I then patched it into my PC and loaded the footage into a movie editing program. I sat and sipped my morning coffee as I reviewed my new footage. It wasn't very entertaining, though, other than the gaunt, gray specter that crept from the kitchen, limped down the corridor, and disappeared into our bedroom. Yes, that had been me as I retired for the evening. Other than that, the camcorder stared unblinking down the hallway for the next forty five minutes or so.

Tick...tock... I soon found it hard to remain focused on my new film. At least my plan worked, I thought. The camera filmed for an entire hour, even if it wasn't producing any evidence. Then it did the strangest thing. It suddenly went out of focus, just as it did the other night. I could hear the whirl of the auto focus as it struggled to film whatever it was seeing. Then it just stopped. This odd behavior lasted for ten seconds or so before the picture came back into focus. The camera worked perfectly for the remainder of the film, just as if nothing odd ever happened.

"Now, that was rather strange," I said to no one. Yes... Rather strange indeed.

~~~~~~~

Fox urine, as odd as this may seem, has long been used by deer hunters to mask human scent. Like the fox, the deer has a very keen sense of smell. It had been my scent that foiled me the evening I spotted them. Now it would be my scent that would lure them to me!

I sprinkled a little on my boots and jacket. I know it sounds
~~~~~~~

gross, but that's nothing compared to the pungent smell. I paused every so often to sprinkle a little of the bottle's contents onto my back trail. As I crossed the creek and neared the vicinity of the presumed den, I sprinkled a tad more pee and then just stood in a thicket, watching…waiting. The trap was set!

The shadows were growing long and it would soon be too dark to see. Then they just appeared in the woodland clearing, silently emerging from the shadows like two gray ghosts. I dared not blink, I stood frozen… For if they spotted me the hunt would be over. They followed my pee-laden trail and were now just a few yards from my hiding place. Curiosity killed the cat, I thought as one of them lowered his head to sniff the pee. I took careful aim. The only sound was a soft click as I eased the hammer back on the single-shot scatter gun.

His head jerked up and his ears rotated as he zeroed in on the strange noise. Then he looked straight at me. KA BOOM! The recoil rocked me backwards as I watched him drop to the ground. At least I got one of the chicken thieves! The woods were silent. As I quickly reloaded I strained to hear the foot falls of the second fox as he fled for his life. The only sound was the ringing in my ears.

I slowly walked into the clearing, squinting to see in the failing light. The corpse lay at my feet. His eyes were wide open as he stared up at me in the gloom. They were lifeless and cold. I then noticed the other fox, lying just a few feet behind him. Yep, it had been a lucky shot. Yes, rather lucky indeed.

~~~~~~~

I spent several hours scrutinizing the footage, trying to see what the camera had not been able to film. The ten seconds of odd behavior was perplexing to say the least. Either something invisible caused it to jump out of focus or it somehow malfunctioned for those few seconds. I didn't think it could have just malfunctioned.
~~~~~~~

Nope, I guessed they had been… Playing with me?

It seemed whatever caused the camera's temporary blindness did not have any intentions of being caught on film. Something had been present in front of the lens and caused the machine to blink, I reasoned. But what? I used the film editing software to isolate the blurry portion of the tape. I then reviewed it frame by frame by frame. There just had to be something there!

The software has a photo feature enabling me to pause the film then take a still shot of the frame, just by clicking the mouse. I proceeded to take a snapshot of each frame on the short clip. I reviewed the pictures one by one, but could not ascertain the cause of the odd behavior. As the film clip neared its end, as the camera was just coming back into focus, I saw them. They formed out of what looked to be the white noise of the camera as it was finally coming back into focus. This fuzz on the film appeared almost as a mist. Yes, my research was producing some haunting results. *Haunting, indeed.*

~~~~~~~

"Stephen, I'm home," my wife called down the dark hallway.

"Come in here and look at this," I called back.

She proceeded down the corridor and into my office. "Look at what?" she inquired.

"A picture of our guests," I replied.

"Guests? Who are you referring to, Stephen?"

"Them," I answered as I pointed at the monitor.

There on my computer screen, staring back at us, were four misty apparitions. They were only visible on that one frame then vanished before the next. An old man stood half in, half out of the open doorway of the guest room. He was hunched over and appeared to be leaning on a walking cane. He had a heavy brow, long thick sideburns and wore suspenders. In the hallway, several
~~~~~~~

feet closer to the camera was a young woman. She had long, dark, flowing hair and was dressed in what looked like an evening gown.

Directly behind her stood a young man. He looked to be around thirty or so. He had his arms around her waist. Because he was standing behind the young lady, I could not see what he was wearing. I could see that he wore glasses, though. Round, black-rimmed glasses. Could this be Andy? She had her head tilted to the right and his tilted to the left. Were they posing for the camera? It certainly appeared as if they were. They were smiling! Then there was the ghostly face of a child. He was much closer to the camera than the others. The transparent face of a young boy. He was just to the left of the shot, a wide grin shown on his face as if he was very happy to be there, in my den.

"Dear God," she whispered. "What have you brought into our house, Stephen?"

"MAPS, I'm sorry we are not available to take your call, leave a message after the beep and we will get back to you," Joe's answering machine assured me.

I had reservations about calling him back after the 'Dear Client, you're crazy' email he sent me. Hell, maybe I was crazy, but I wanted to prove to him I was not just hearing things.

"Joe, this is Steve" I stated. "I'm sorry to bother you, but I think I now have evidence that will substantiate my claims of activity." "Please get back to me… Goodbye" I hung up. At least I considered my new film footage to be evidence. It proved, at least as far as I was concerned, that whispering ghosts were indeed roaming my house at night. Scaring my wife and posing for my video camera. *Yep, I'll show him who's crazy! Crazy… Indeed!*

'Purgatory is the condition or process of purification in which the souls of those who die in a state of grace are made ready for Heaven. This is an idea that has ancient roots and is well-attested in early Christian literature, while the conception of purgatory as a geographically situated place is largely the achievement of medieval Christian piety and imagination. John Wesley, the founder of Methodism, believed in an intermediate state between death and the final judgment and in the possibility of 'continuing to grow in holiness there,' but Methodism does not officially affirm his belief and denies the possibility of helping by prayer any who may be in that state.' *Now this is interesting,* I thought as I read the online Wikipedia article. *Pray... Pray for me,* I reflected as I read the words.

Could this have something to do with the *prison* referred to in the book of Peter? Something to do with my research? "The notion of purgatory is associated particularly with the Latin Rite of the Catholic Church." The article read. I glanced at the clock to see it was after midnight. Time flies when you're reading. I found the article to be very interesting indeed. 'The word purgatory has come to refer also to a wide range of historical and modern conceptions of postmortem suffering short of everlasting damnation, and is used, in a non-specific sense, to mean any place or condition of suffering or torment, especially one that is temporary.' The article concluded.

Could this be the Catholic version of an *in-between*? Did they believe to be fact, what the Pastor dismissed as my insanity? 'Postmortem suffering short of eternal damnation' seemed to certainly fit with my theory. My thoughts were soon interrupted by my wife calling my name.

"Stephen."

"Yes... I'll be there in a moment," I called back across the hallway. She woke up and wondered why I wasn't yet in bed. I had been keeping rather long hours lately. Yes, rather long hours, indeed. My research demanded it!

CHAPTER SEVEN

"Saint Luke's, how may I help you?" The voice inquired.

"Is the Father in?" I asked.

"No sir," the voice replied. "Father Jim is on retreat until Friday. May I take a message?"

Crap, I thought. *Just my luck! There's never a priest around when you need one*. I chuckled to myself. "Sure," I said and gave her my name and number. "Thank you, goodbye." I hung up.

I was almost glad Father Jim had not been in his office. I was not really sure what I wished to ask him. *Does a madman question his own sanity? Do the dead speak, or am I just crazy, Father?* I imagined myself inquiring of him. Would he dismiss my research as lunacy as the youth Pastor had done? Or would the teachings of his doctrine allow the possibility there is a purgatory, a place…*in-between*? I would have to wait until Friday to find out.

I still had not heard back from Joe and MAPS. The list of folks who thought I was crazy seemed to be growing. I even had my own doubts. But I did have the phantom voices on tape. *Pray for me. We're not dead! We cursed at God!* Maybe…I wasn't so crazy after all, I reasoned. My thoughts were then interrupted by a faint tug on my shirt. I spun in my chair to find no one was there.

"Pray… Pray for me!" They requested prayer, so perhaps prayer was the reason they were here. I planned to conduct another experiment later that evening. My research demanded it!

Lynn called to inform me she had been asked to work late, so Cruzer and I had the house to ourselves. *"Our Father who art in Heaven,"* I listened to my reciting of the Lord's Prayer on my new recorder. *"Hallowed be Thy name."*

Tick…tock… I could here the mantle clock counting the seconds in the background. *"Thy Kingdom come,* tick…tock… *Thy will be done,* tick…tock… *On Earth as it is in Heaven.*" I stood in the den, my head bowed, the lights extinguished. Tick…tock… I had continued my heartfelt prayer to its conclusion. *"Amen."* Tick…tock… The recording was nearing its end. My ears strained to hear the slightest sound.

A spine numbing chill ran down my back as I fumbled to rewind the recorder. Tick…tock… A dark voice confirmed that at least someone had, indeed, heard my prayer.

"Pray sucker… Praaay!" The phantom voice whispered into the microphone.

Yep… Something answered me and it didn't sound like God.

'Think your home is haunted?' The website read. 'Contact Gabreael. A light in an ever darkening world. Over twenty years of experience in paranormal investigation.' The site didn't list a phone number, but rather an email address. Additional information on the web page revealed she was located over four hours away from my sleepy little town. But she was in the same state, at least.

I didn't think my house was haunted, I knew it was. I still had not heard back from MAPS and it seemed as if they were avoiding me. I needed some form of validation, someone who would listen to my new claims of activity. Someone to help me understand just who, or *what*, we were now living with. I couldn't expect her to drive for four hours one way just to help me, a total stranger. But maybe she would listen and not just dismiss me as a nut case.

Only one way to find out, I concluded. I clicked on the email link and attached the misty photo I took two nights before. I also decided to attach an EVP. *You must help us... We're not dead* had been my selection. I then typed a brief message.

> *Dear Gabreael,*
>
> *Please find attached an EVP that was recorded in a local graveyard while conducting some research. Also attached is a photo that was taken in my home earlier this week. I think that my house is in fact haunted. If you think that you can help us please respond.*
>
> *Best regards,*
>
> *Steve.*

I wondered what sort of response I would get from her as I clicked on the "send" button, then popped a sleeping pill and retired for the evening.

~~~~~~~

Ring... Ring... ring!

"Answer the damn phone, Lynn," I muttered, still deep in the grasp of my dreamless coma.

Ring... Ring!

I opened my eyes to see Cruzer lying beside me in her place. The clock on the nightstand said I slept past mid-morning again.
~~~~~~~

Lynn was already at work and sleeping beauty didn't look like he was planning to answer it. He growled in protest as I reached across the bed and grabbed the cordless phone.

"Hello?" I groggily answered.

"Yes, Steve?" The voice inquired.

"Yes… This is Steve" I replied, trying my best to sound coherent.

"This is Father Jim and I'm returning your call," the kindly voice informed me.

"Yes, Father Jim… I wanted to talk with you about something that has been weighing on my mind lately. Thanks for calling me back," I told him, trying not to sound too distraught.

"Are you a member here at Saint Luke's?" he wanted to know.

"No Father," I replied. I used to be of the Presbyterian faith… But not anymore." There was a brief pause.

"Would you like to come by my office and talk with me?" He finally asked.

"Yes, Father, I certainly would," I stated, hoping my previous statement hadn't sounded as crazy to him as it had to me.

"Would six Monday evening be all right with you?" he suggested.

"Yes, Father, six on Monday evening would be just fine, indeed." I assured him. *Well, here we go again,* I thought as I reflected back on my last theological debate. Would Father Jim be receptive in regards to my research, open to my theories… Or would his name be added to the list? I would have to wait until Monday to find out.

My thoughts were soon interrupted by a very cold, wet nose on my elbow. "Damn it, Cruzer!" I swore.

"You've got mail," the voice alerted me. The email was from Gabreael, I noticed as I glanced at the monitor.

Hi Steve,

If you will send me your phone number, I will call you this evening. I look forward to talking with you.

Sincerely,

Gabreael.

The note read. I replied with my number and anxiously awaited her call. *A light in an ever darkening world*, her website promised. Maybe she could shed some light into the darkness in which we now resided. Maybe she could illuminate the shadows and dark whispers haunting my wife and me for the past few weeks. I didn't know, but I certainly hoped so.

CHAPTER EIGHT

Yes, my wife and I experienced many odd occurrences in our home recently. The shadow man, the whispering voices, the tugs on our clothing, and the posing apparitions in the photo. The thing that bothered me the most about that picture was the little ghost boy. Why would a child be present in a realm for unclean souls? What could he have possibly done in his short time here on this earth that would prevent him from entering the gates of heaven?

I always assumed all children had a free pass through those pearly gates when they prematurely departed this world. Was he somehow paying for the sins of his parents? Assuming the young couple in the photo were his parents. Was he here because he was too young to comprehend the gospel? Were there more lost children hanging around the cemetery, trapped somewhere *in-between*? Only one way to find out, I thought. My research demanded it!

~~~~~~~

"Are there any children present here?" I asked as I nervously
~~~~~~~

glanced around the graveyard. "Why aren't they in Heaven?" I waited. "Are they trapped here?" If my questions were being answered, I could not hear them. I didn't really care if anyone saw me there, in the cemetery this time. The church custodian thought I was some kind of mad Genealogist. The young Pastor thought I was just mad… Period. "How many children are here?"

"Get out!" the voice answered.

What the hell? I must have jumped a foot off the ground.

"You get out!"

I quickly spun around to find no one there. Not a living soul—just rows of cold stone. "Holy shit!" I exclaimed out loud. It was time for me to make a hasty exit. Yes, rather hasty, indeed! The disembodied whispers in my ear again caused my skin to crawl! *Damn, I hope I caught that on my recorder,* I thought as I climbed into my truck and sped the hell away from there.

~~~~~~~

I spent the remainder of the afternoon carefully reviewing my new recording, finding it hard to shake the eerie sensation that caused me to flee. Yes, it had been a frightening experience, to say the least. I hadn't just imagined the angry voice, though. It was right there on my recorder and it sounded really pissed!

Apparently, my questions had been on a rather touchy subject. One they did not wish to discuss. The recorder contained another warning however. One I did not audibly hear when I was at the cemetery. "Why aren't they in Heaven?" I rewound to listen again.

"You are dead now, spirit man!" the voice stated.

"Spirit man?" I repeated to myself. Was he talking to me? I reflected back on the comic book heroes of my youth. "Never fear, Spirit Man is here!" I grinned as I imagined myself as some supernatural comic book character. Speeding along in my spook mobile, racing from mild insanity to sheer madness at the speed of
~~~~~~~

light. My grin soon faded however as I then heard something I previously missed.

"Fear the Demons," the voice faintly whispered shortly before it sent me scurrying to leave.

Was this another warning? I feared it was. My thoughts were soon interrupted by the ringing of the telephone.

~~~~~~~~

"Hello" I grabbed it on the second ring.

"Yes, is this Steve?" The voice inquired. "This is Gabreael," she stated.

I thanked her for taking her time to call me.

"Tell me more about your experiences," she said.

"Okay," I replied. She listened patiently as I recounted the haunting events one by one. I informed her of my research. I told her about the investigation conducted by MAPS and how they now didn't return my calls. I related how my conversation with the Pastor caused me to question my own beliefs, my own sanity.

"Hang on just a moment," she suddenly interrupted.

I thought I could hear her writing something down on paper. Was she filling in the client questionnaire? I hoped not. Would she also find me guilty by reason of insanity?

"I know what's going on with you," she said after several seconds. "It just came to me."

"Came to you?" I asked her. "What do you mean by… Came to you?"

"I am a medium," she replied. "The spirits in your home have followed you there."

No shit, Sherlock! I thought. *Hell, I knew that... And I wasn't even a medium!*

"Your house isn't haunted."

"Oh, yes it is," I insisted.
~~~~~~~~

"No, it is not… Just listen to me. You are a haunted person," she explained. "They would not be in your home if it were not for you. You attract them, like metal shavings to a magnet. You are a natural born empath," she informed me.

"A natural born what?" I asked her to repeat herself, not sure if I was hearing her correctly.

"You're an Empath," she said. "It's a sixth sense, look it up!"

"So… You're telling me I have a sixth sense... Which I have possessed since birth?" I prodded.

"Yes, that's what natural born means," she said. "Your ability is of a very high degree."

"Ability?" I repeated the word. "What sort of ability?"

"Your ability to communicate," she further enlightened me.

My mind whirled as it tried to make some sense out of this madness. *My ability to communicate? With whom, the dead? Why would I be given such a morbid talent?* For what purpose…for what reason? It seemed beyond my comprehension. "Why should I even believe any of this?" *Oops, did I say that out loud?*

Then she said something that caused me to reconsider her clairvoyant abilities. "What's this addiction you have, if you don't mind my asking?"

My response had been a hesitant pause.

"Yes, I'm seeing some sort of addiction," she continued. "Would you care to tell me about it?" she asked.

"Oh…ah… I don't know what you're talking about," I lied as I glanced down at the quickly dwindling supply of pain pills there on my desk. Was I addicted? I hadn't mentioned my surgery. *How in the hell could she know?* I wondered. *Can you even lie to a medium?* She went on to tell me other things about myself. Things she couldn't possibly have known.

~~~~~~~
~~~~~~~

'An empath or telempath is a person who has an acute or highly developed sense of empathy. In the paranormal and in some works of science fiction and fantasy, empathy is a paranormal or psychic ability to sense the emotions of others. It is distinguished from telepathy, which allows one to perceive thoughts as well. Occasionally empaths are also able to project their own emotions, or to affect the emotions of others.' Wikipedia kept me up late again, reading about this mysterious sixth sense Gabreael claimed I possessed since birth.

Psychic ability to sense the emotions of others. Could this mean I was actually a psychic? Psychotic, I might have believed, but I didn't believe in psychics… Or mediums, for that matter. Then another thought occurred to me. *Hell, I hadn't believed in ghosts either, until I photographed the wispy phantoms in my den.* Yes, seeing is believing, they say. And the photo, along with the other things we had seen and heard, definitely made believers out of Lynn and I.

In the paranormal and in some works of science fiction and fantasy the article read. I knew the occurrences in our home were not fantasy or fiction, so they must be…paranormal, I concluded. Another question came to mind, a question I asked Gabreael. *Why me? Why was I chosen to receive this gift…this sixth sense?*

"Everything happens for a reason," had been her reply.

I have always known I was somehow different than most normal folks. I always perceived myself as being maybe just a little odd or strange compared to others and Gabreael touched on this fact during our conversation.

"You are a very emotionally sensitive person" she stated.

That was true enough and I had never been able to understand why I felt the way I sometimes feel. Sudden bouts of anger, sadness, or depression would sometimes plummet me into a state of despair. I could never put my finger on the cause of these emotions and it seemed as if they were not my own at times. And another weird but true fact is I can tell if a person is lying just by hearing the tone of their voice as they speak, even if I just met them. Body language was another specialty of mine. I always just thought of myself as being very perceptive…not psychic. I thought back on my conversation with the young Pastor. He said he didn't think I was crazy. He was lying. I could hear it in his voice and read it in his expressions, long before he confirmed my intuitions by his haste to be rid of me.

Gabreael also touched on some other truths about my life. She pointed out my love for animals, especially dogs. This was also accurate as I do love animals, especially Cruzer, who I raised from a pup. It seemed most of her statements had been relative to the living, though, as accurate as they had been. Except the one she made in reference to my abilities to communicate with the dead. Could my empathy reach across the invisible borders between the living and the deceased? Apparently this was so, judging from my photo and the shadowy, whispering voices on my recorder.

She went on to tell me other facts about myself. I was basically a loner, although I felt as if I were never alone. The fact I just can't bear for anyone to be angry at me, and I go out of my way not to hurt anyone's feelings. But one statement she made held more meaning to me than any other. Finally, someone spoke the words I so needed to hear.

"Yes I believe you… No, you are not crazy."

Fear the Demons. I had written the words down on my notepad, just another piece to my macabre puzzle. The apparitions that appeared in my photo looked to be a rather happy lot. Other than the fact they were dead and in my living room, they didn't seem too scary at all. They certainly did not look evil. The shadow man appeared only to my wife and he was not using a walking cane, so I figured the old man in the photo could not be him either. So who was the shadow man?

Gabreael advised me to just ignore them all. She said that by attempting to film and record them, I was giving them encouragement to communicate.

Easy for her to say, I thought. She wasn't living here in their midst. I decided to take her advice though in hopes that maybe… they would just leave.

CHAPTER NINE

"Is Father Jim in?" I asked his secretary. "I believe he is expecting me."

"Yes sir, follow me," she replied as she rose from her desk and led me down the corridor.

Father Jim was a kindly looking, older gentleman. He must have been around sixty five or so.

"Yes, Stephen, come in," he greeted me.

"I am so glad you could meet with me, Father," I replied as we shook hands and he asked me to have a seat.

"So, you informed me you were once of the Presbyterian faith?" he started off the conversation. "What denomination are you now?"

I hadn't expected this to be such a difficult question. "Well… I am not sure, Father," had been my eventual reply.

"Please, tell me what is troubling you, my son," he urged.

"Do you believe in life after death?" I asked him.

"Yes" he replied. "Eternal life through God's salvation," he stated.

"So the spirit lives on after the body is dust?" I asked.

"Yes, most certainly we do," he replied.

"So… You believe in heaven and hell?" I inquired. "Angels and demons?"

"Yes, most definitely. What do you believe, Stephen?"

Damn it, another question I really didn't have an answer for. *Well, here goes*, I thought. "I believe in…ghosts, Father." I finally answered as I studied the expression on his face. It was an expression of concern. Concern for what… My sanity? "They…talk to me, Father."

"Continue, my son," he encouraged.

He sat patiently as I told him everything, from the beginning. I also told him of my conversation with Gabreael and my newly discovered sixth sense.

"Is there a place such as the book of Peter refers to, Father?" I finally asked him. I sat there awaiting his reply, hoping my confession hadn't sounded as crazy to him as it had to me.

"Well, yes… There must be," he thoughtfully responded.

"Could these be the same spirits now residing in my house?"

"You said you have their voices on tape."

"Yes, I do, Father. Would you like to hear them?" I suggested.

"No," he replied. "That will not be necessary. You said you have a photo of them also?" he inquired.

"Yes, Father, taken in my den. Would you like to see it?"

"No," was again his reply. "The fact you are here and seeking my help is proof enough," he assured me.

"So… You do believe me Father?" I prodded as I stared into his sincere, blue eyes.

"Yes, Stephen… I believe you."

~~~~~~~

Well, that went rather well, I thought to myself as I climbed into my truck and headed home. *Yes, rather well indeed!*

Fear the Demons, are the words that now had me worried. Fear was the one thing I seemed to have no shortage of lately.

Father Jim ended my visit with a prayer of protection. He offered to call the diocese and inquire if they had an exorcist available anywhere near our area.

"An exorcist?" I asked him. Did he think I was possessed?

"No," he answered. The diocese has certain priests appointed by the Catholic Church to deal with the demonic. Father Jim had been approved to perform house blessings, not to banish demons. "I am afraid a house blessing may just make matters worse," he explained. If, in fact, I was dealing with a demon.

Unlike the Presbyterians and the teachings of the Pastor, the teachings of the Catholic faith allowed the possibility there is a realm somewhere *in-between*. And also in the existence of angels and demons. This theology made more sense to me. After all, if there are angels who serve in Heaven, there must be demons who serve in Hell. If one exists, then surely does the other. If not, why would the Catholic Church have appointed certain priests to deal with those from down under? Was the shadow man a demon? He had no smiling face like the spirits in my picture. He had no wings, my wife had said. Father Jim must have thought so, judging by his prayer of protection and his suggestion that it might require an exorcism to be rid of it.

"Father, what in the hell have I brought into our house?" I asked him.

"In religion, folklore, and mythology a demon (or daemon, dæmon, daimon from Greek: δαίμων daimōn) is a supernatural being generally described as a malevolent spirit. In Christian terms,
~~~~~~~

demons are generally understood as fallen angels, formerly of God. A demon is frequently depicted as a force that may be conjured and insecurely controlled."

"Conjured?" I uttered aloud as I read the Wikipedia definition of the word. I had not been attempting to *conjure* anything. I was conducting research, not conjuring demons. Had my research unleashed one of Hell's minions that was lurking there, in that quiet place of the dead? I was afraid it just might have.

Or… Was the voice referring to the demons we all face in this realm? The realm of the living. *We all have our demons,* I thought as I popped another pain pill and lit another smoke.

I promised Gabreael I would heed her advice and try to ignore them. However, this was proving to be a rather difficult task. Yes… rather difficult indeed! It seemed our invisible guests were seeking our attention. Judging by the persistent tugs and the occasional whispers we were still experiencing, they had no plans to leave. Then something happened late one evening to convince me I could not ignore them any longer.

~~~~~~~

I was up late again, pursuing my course of study online. The door to my office slowly creaked open to reveal my wife standing there in the doorway.

"Yes dear, I'll be to bed shortly" I said to her. I received no reply. "Lynn? What's wrong honey?" I asked.

Still no answer. I noticed *something* was wrong. Very wrong! She stood in the doorway with a blank expression, staring at nothing. She seemed to be looking right through me.

"Stay out," she said in a voice not quite her own.

"Stay out?" I asked her, trying to understand what she was telling me. No reply. "Stay out of where?" I prodded.

"The graveyard," she whispered.
~~~~~~~

What the hell? Was she sleepwalking? She seemed to be in a trance. *Knowledge can be painful* again flashed through my mind as I stared into those empty blue eyes. They were lifeless and cold.

"Lynn… Honey, wake up," I told her.

She let out a heavy sigh as I rose from my chair and approached her, our eyes still locked in that unearthly gaze. Taking her by the shoulders, I gave her a gentle shake. "Lynn?" I could see the light slowly come back into her eyes.

"What are you doing, Stephen?" She asked in her own confused voice. "Why did you wake me?"

"Go back to bed, now" I told her. I led her into the bedroom and tucked her in. I wasn't sure what caused her mysterious behavior, but I did know I never wanted to see that expression again.

That empty stare and her trancelike tone still haunt me now. I went back into my office and closed the door. I would not sleep tonight. Nope… Not after witnessing that. I sat for several minutes staring at the voice recorder lying on my desk. Hesitantly, I picked it up and pushed the record button.

"What in the hell do you want from us?" I demanded. "You leave her out of this, do you understand me?" I growled. If my questions were being answered, I could not hear them. "Leave her alone, God damn it!" I swore. Now it was I who was pissed!

"Your fear can't protect you," was the only response as I played back the recording.

My wife apparently had no recollection of her midnight wanderings. I thought it best not to mention her sleepwalking episode. She had enough worries as it was and I didn't want her sanity to become one of them.

"Didn't you come to bed last night?" she asked.

"No honey, I slept here in my chair," I replied, my neck stiff and my back aching. This wasn't a lie as I had, in fact, fallen asleep in my chair. "Did you sleep well?" I asked.

"Yes, like a baby," she assured me as she kissed me on the cheek and headed off to work.

I hadn't slept well, however. I sat up for most of the night. My senses fully alert, my ears strained to hear the slightest sound. I was unable to rest after the zombie-like visit from my wife of almost thirty years. I had never known her to sleep walk before. Something caused it, I reasoned. Could the cause have been stress? Lord knows, she had been through a lot recently. Or could it have been something else? *Something...unseen?* Was this a plea... Or another warning? *Maybe I should take her advice,* I thought. *Maybe I should stay out of the graveyard.*

CHAPTER TEN

A week passed since my visit with Father Jim. I was hoping he would call and let me know if a Pope-appointed priest was available in my area. I still wasn't sure of exactly what I was dealing with.

I talked with Gabreael in the interim, informing her of the *ghost walk* Lynn had taken and of the *fear can't protect you* EVP I recorded just after.

"Human spirits are of free will," she enlightened me. "They cannot be ousted by religious provocation. If you, in fact, do have a demonic entity, it won't be easy to get rid of," she advised. The thing that now worried her was the odd behavior of my spouse. "I do have access to a demonologist," she offered. "She has assisted me on cases in the past. Why don't I have Sister call you?" she asked.

"Sister?" I replied.

"She is a Greek Orthodox Nun being appointed by her church."

Dear God, I thought. "Do you feel that a demonologist is required?" I questioned.

"It's better to be safe than sorry," was her reply.

Your fear can't protect you, I reflected back on the whispered statement and wondered what could protect us. How do you fight something you cannot see? Apparently, whatever this was could see us. It appeared to be watching Lynn on the two occasions it had shown itself. I hadn't planned on involving her in my research, but the shadow man apparently had other plans. Then there was the revelation of my sixth sense. I was still struggling with the concept. *Ability to communicate with the dead* is what Gabreael claimed. If I, in fact, have this ability then maybe I could use it to find more answers. My thoughts were soon interrupted by the ringing of the telephone.

"Stephen?" the voice inquired. "This is Father Jim."

"Hello, Father Thank you for getting back to me. Do you have any news for me?" I asked.

"Yes" he answered, "But I am afraid it isn't the news you were hoping for."

"Then the Diocese has no Exorcist in our area, Father?"

"No, I'm afraid not," he replied.

Shit! I thought to myself. *There's never an exorcist around when you really need one.*

"I would be glad to perform a house blessing for you, but that is about all I can do," he offered. "However, it would have to wait for a couple of weeks," he informed me. "My schedule is rather full these days."

"I understand," I told him. At least he was willing to try to help me after hearing my ludicrous sounding story. That was more than I could say for MAPS and the Pastor. "Father Jim, would you be willing to guide me if I should decide to perform my own house blessing?" I inquired.

"Yes, Steve" he immediately replied. "Of course I would be willing to assist you in any way I can."

"Great… Thanks, Father, I would really appreciate your guidance."

They would not be in your home it if were not for you, Gabreael advised. If I was the reason they were here then wasn't it up to me to depart them? If my sixth sense was to communicate with the dead then maybe it could be used to some advantage. If it brought them here… Then maybe it could also get rid of them. My thoughts were soon interrupted by a very cold, wet nose on my elbow. "Damn it Cruzer!" I swore.

~~~~~~~

"Don't be late for your doctor's appointment," the voice spoke through the fog of the sleeping pills.

"Yes, dear," I replied. I slowly staggered into the bathroom and took a good, long look at myself in the mirror. A tired and confused old man stared back at me. He had a haunted look in his still medicated brown eyes. They were lifeless and cold. Gabreael mentioned she had seen an addiction. I denied any knowledge of this fact. The old man in the mirror couldn't be fooled though, for he knew the truth. I could see it in his lifeless stare…in those empty, bag-laden eyes. Yes, she had been accurate about that as well. Yes… Rather accurate indeed. I wasn't going to tell her, though.

It wasn't my fault I was dependant on the pills. I was just following doctor's orders. It wasn't like I was abusing the medications as I was following the prescribed dosages. *Should I tell her the truth?* I thought. She was nice enough to try to help me. Perhaps the problem was I didn't want to acknowledge the fact I was becoming addicted. Yes… The old man in the mirror knew the
~~~~~~~

truth. "She already knows," he silently informed me, our eyes still locked in that unearthly gaze.

Yes, my life had changed dramatically over the past few weeks. It seemed my research indeed led me to revise some facts and form a few new theories. I reflected back on the events that took place as a result. Yes… My life changed in ways unimaginable. My research compelled me to change my religious beliefs. It had in fact, changed my outlook on everything I believed prior to all of this. I never believed in ghosts, now my house was haunted. I never believed in mediums, now I sat anxiously by the phone hoping Gabreael would call. I never believed in psychic powers either, but now I was told I have possessed them since birth.

If the young Pastor had not dismissed me as just a crazy old man, would my research have changed his beliefs? *If he only knew*, I thought. Would he also no longer be of the Presbyterian faith? Would he then believe the teachings of his doctrine were incorrect? That there is a realm *in-between*, filled with the restless souls of those either lost or trapped?

I thought about an atheist friend of mine. Would the findings of my research change his view on religion? He apparently had none. We just live our mundane lives, aging as we spin on this third rock from the sun. Then we just die—no spirit to dwell or linger on, in this or any other realm. We are here by happenstance with no purpose other than survival and greed. *If he only knew,* I thought. *Dear God…if he only knew.*

I said the shadow man had no wings, so he could not be an angel. *Do all angels have wings?* I pondered. Reflection back on an event from my childhood caused me to doubt that belief. After all, I had seen and talked to one on that hot summer night, or at least I always thought so. I must have been around eleven or so at the time. He didn't appear to have wings, though. He wore blue jeans and a white tee shirt.

~~~~~~~~

We were returning from an afternoon of visiting my grandparents who lived just a few miles away from us. My stepmother sat in the front, holding my little brother on her lap. My younger sister and I sat in the back seat of our family station wagon, wishing it had air conditioning. Like I said, it was hot and we had all the windows rolled down. This was long before the days of mandatory seatbelts and the *click it or ticket* laws of today. I can't recall if the wagon even had seatbelts, but if it did no one thought to wear them.

I can remember seeing the flash of headlights as the sports car ran through the stop sign. My stepmother screamed as it broadsided us at over seventy miles an hour. Then the sound of glass exploding and metal smashing as our car rolled over several times, coming to rest on its top in an overgrown field. Then there was silence. The next thing I remember was two arms reaching through the window to gently pull me from the wreckage. He was a teenage boy who looked to be around seventeen or so. He helped me to my feet, placing an arm around me.

"It's okay," he comforted me. "Everything is going to be fine."

I felt no pain. We slowly walked around the car, surveying the carnage. The scene had a surreal feeling, almost as if it were a dream. I didn't see how everything could be fine, though. I could see my stepmother lying half-in and half-out of the open door of the over turned wagon. She didn't appear to be moving.

"Momma!" I shouted, fearing she was dead. I had already suffered the loss of my birth mother at the tender age of six. She had been killed in a terrible accident while returning home from a shopping trip with a girlfriend.

"It's okay," he again assured me. "Everything will be just fine."
~~~~~~~~

The next thing I remember was the sound of sirens. I opened my eyes to see bright lights and strange faces hovering over me. I fought to comprehend what was happening. "It's okay, kid. Everything is going to be fine," the voice told me. "You have been in an accident and we are on the way to the hospital. I didn't feel fine, though. My head felt as if it had been hit with a sledge hammer. The attendant was wiping my forehead and I could see the fresh blood stains on the white towel.

I was examined at the hospital by the emergency room physician, then treated and released later that night. I could hear him informing my father of my condition. "He has a mild concussion and multiple contusions, but no broken bones. I have removed several fragments of glass from his forehead and sutured his wounds."

I had received over a hundred stitches.

"You will need to keep a close eye on him for the next few days. If he has any episodes of blurred vision or dizziness, get him back in here immediately. You said he was ejected from the vehicle?" He questioned my father.

"Yes, we were both thrown from the car. When I came to, he was lying on the ground beside me," my father answered, with the look of shock still on his face. "I was afraid he was dead."

"It's a miracle either of you escaped without more serious injuries."

"Yes," my dad agreed. "It was a miracle."

My step mother survived, but spent many months confined to a hospital bed. She crushed several vertebrae in her spine. My sister also received a concussion in the accident, along with many cuts, bumps, and bruises. She was released a couple of days after the crash. My little brother suffered much more serious head trauma than my sister and I, and spent almost a month in intensive care.

Father escaped with only a busted lip.

I watched as the doctor sewed him up. My Dad is one of the toughest men I have ever known. The doctor was preparing to give him a shot to numb him before the sewing started.

"That won't be necessary." He never even blinked as the physician performed his handy work. He just sat there on the edge of the operating table with an empty look in his eyes, no expression on his face. I never mentioned the dark-eyed, young man who pulled me from the crumpled station wagon. I knew I hadn't just imagined him, though. He must have been an angel, I have always thought. *Maybe he had been my guardian angel. Had I cheated death that night?*

I wasn't certain, but I couldn't help think I just might have. The accident took place on a desolate country crossroads. There were no houses in the immediate vicinity, no convenience stores, or no Kentucky Fried, Taco Bell that exist there today. It was just a lonely *X* in the middle of nowhere. Where had my mysterious friend come from? Where could he have gone? His memory has haunted me over the forty plus years that have passed since that night. Maybe one day we will meet again. I've always hoped so.

CHAPTER ELEVEN

I still needed to find out exactly who, *or what,* we were dealing with here. I wondered what advice the Nun would give me when she called. Gabreael warned me that in the Sister's view, anything not of heaven must surely be from hell. She apparently doesn't believe in ghosts or human spirits, just demons, which was her specialty.

Everyone has their specialty, I thought. Even if it takes them fifty years to discover what it might be. Mine was to communicate with the dead, apparently, so that's what I thought I should do. I decided another experiment was in order. My research demanded it! Besides, they were already here and making themselves known to us. *What could it hurt?* I had been hunting them at night and got the hell scared out of me in the process.

The scariest thing though, was the late night visit from the living dead. Yes, my wife's midnight appearance had been the most disturbing thing I witnessed thus far. That distant stare and the creepy voice sent chills down my spine. Nope, I never want to witness that again. I would have to get rid of them… If I could only find out what they wanted. I could not find the answers without recording them. I formulated a new plan.

Soon after Lynn departed for work I made myself a pot of coffee and sat down at the kitchen table with my voice recorder. "Anybody want coffee?" I said to no one in particular. I wasn't sure if they would answer, but I thought it was worth a shot. They could apparently see and hear, so why not taste and smell? I paused for a few seconds to give anyone who wished to speak time to do so. I then rewound and listened for a possible reply.

"YESSSS!" The phantom voice whispered.

I hit record. "Who's here with me now?" I casually inquired.

"Carol," was the faint reply. She sounded like a young lady. Could this be the gown-clad apparition in my photo?

"Hi, Carol," I said. "Could you please tell me why you are here?"

Nothing, no reply.

"Do you need prayer?" I listened in anticipation.

"Give us some power," was her request.

"What do you mean, *power*?" I inquired, having no idea what she could be referring to.

"We need your power," was her whispered reply.

"My power? What kind of *power?*" I prodded.

The next voice did not sound like Carol. It was an angry, impatient sounding male whisper.

"I want it now!" had been the only reply.

"And who are you, sir?" I asked. I could hear nothing other than my own voice on the recorder. "Carol, who was that?" I questioned hoping to get a response.

"ANDY TURNER!" The male voice shouted over mine as I

was asking her the question.

"Andy, are you a human spirit or…inhuman?"

There was no reply. The conversation was apparently over.

~~~~~~~~

"Could the shadow man be a demon?" I asked the question to the Nun who called later that evening.

"They are all demonic," had been her reply. Gabreael had forwarded her my EVP captures and ghost photo for her review, prior to the phone call. "You must take the necessary precautions to protect yourself," she insisted.

"What sort of precautions, Sister?" I asked her.

"Get a pen and write down what I am about to tell you," she instructed. She gave me a rather lengthy list of scripture verses. Yes, rather lengthy indeed. I wrote them down, one by one. "Read those verses aloud morning, noon, and night. Do not try to communicate with them," she advised.

"You mean I should not record them, Sister?"

"No, not under any circumstances." she replied. "You will only read the verses I gave you. It is imperative you do exactly as I say." She then went on to enlighten me with her insight into my situation.

"Why are they here, Sister?" I wanted to know.

"They are after your soul," she informed me. "They are there to disrupt your sleep, to drain you of your energy, to drag you down, to make you doubt your own sanity," she stated.

"Well, they're doing a damn fine job so far," I admitted as I thought back on the events of the past few weeks. Yes, my sleep had been disrupted and my energy was drained. *Does a mad man realize he is insane?* I reflected back on the question I still had no answer for.

"They will kill the dog," she warned after I mentioned Cruzer's odd behavior.
~~~~~~~~

"Why would they hurt Cruzer?" I asked.

"Because he protects you," was her reply.

The thought of this caused me to fear for him. I think more of that mutt than I do most people I've known. "I will tell them to leave my dog and my wife out of this," I angrily said.

"You will not speak to them, Stephen!" she admonished.

"But I must!" I argued. My research demanded it!

"No you *MUST* not talk to them," she repeated. "I am going to give you a list of items you will need in order to protect yourself. When you have every item on the list, call me back."

The hour long conversation ended with my assurance that I would follow her advice. *What she doesn't know won't hurt me*, I thought to myself as I hung up the phone. I just couldn't believe the smiling group in my photo could be evil. The shadow man on the other hand, was still uncategorized as far as I was concerned. *Don't talk to the demons,* the Nun warned. *Okay, I won't talk to the demon*, I thought. *I'll just talk to my new friends, the Turners, who joined me in my kitchen for coffee earlier.* After all…my research demanded it.

~~~~~~~

Yes, my research indeed changed my life. I made many new acquaintances while conducting it. The Pastor, a priest, the ghost busters, a medium, and a demon-stalking Nun were among the living. The Turner's, the shadow man, an elderly gentleman, and the little ghost boy were among the deceased. This might make a great book someday, I thought. What might I title it? *Empath without a Clue* seemed to fit. I shook my head in disbelief as I wondered how my life could possibly get any weirder than in the last month. *Does a madman question his own sanity?* I still didn't know the answer, but if it turned out to be yes, then I had a good excuse. Yes, a very good excuse…indeed! My thoughts were then
~~~~~~~

interrupted by a faint tug on my collar. I paid it no notice this time. I didn't even bother to turn around, for I already knew no one was there.

We need your power was the reply Carol gave me when I asked why they were here. I had no idea what sort of *power* she referred to, though. Did I actually possess some sort of *power* they wished to draw from me? Could that explain the drained feeling I experienced as of late? And why do they need power? For what purpose? *Just more damn questions,* I thought.

Maybe my new medium friend could shed some light on this matter. I would have to ask her the next time she called. The Nun's shopping list was a rather bizarre one to say the least. I had no idea where I might procure the items. Holy water, salt from the Dead Sea, blessed frankincense, blessed white candles, and five rosaries were not the kind of items you can find at the local five and dime. Sister directed me to an online store operated by the Benedictine Monks. They would have the rosaries she requested.

While I conducted my virtual shopping spree, I noticed they also had pet medals blessed with a prayer of protection. Cruzer wasn't Catholic, but I figured it might not be a bad idea. The Monks didn't offer overnight shipping, so I could expect to receive my merchandise in five to seven business days. The holy water was a no brainer as Saint Luke's had a fountain full of it in the sanctuary. Sister advised me that blessed kosher salt would suffice if I couldn't find any from the Dead Sea. That just left the candles, the incense, and a priest who was willing to bless all of it.

I would have to put a call into Father Jim. Gabreael stated human spirits were of free will and could not be ousted by religious provocation. I wasn't really worried about human spirits. Now that I was beginning to accept the fact they were here, I wasn't even scared of them anymore. If my ability was to communicate with the dead, I better get used to them. The threat of a dog killing, wife stalking demon scared the hell out of me, though. If the shadow man was demonic, then he would have to go.

"Yea though I walk through the valley," I recited the scripture verses from the Nun's top forty list just as I had each day since our phone conversation. *Morning, noon, and night* she instructed. I felt rather foolish, though, sitting there reading Bible verses to the dog. The look he gave me seemed to confirm he felt the same way. I'm an Empath, not a priest.

"For this reason was the gospel also preached to them that are dead." I reflected on the words of Peter. Maybe the verses would be beneficial to the human spirits here as well as *insecurely control* the demonic. *A paranormal or psychic ability to sense the emotions of others*, the Wikipedia article stated. What I had been feeling lately was hard for me to put my finger on. It wasn't so much a feeling of emotion, but rather a feeling of dread. The air seemed to suddenly grow heavy at times. I could feel a dark presence whenever this would occur. A feeling of anger would sometimes come with it.

Maybe I better keep reading like the Nun instructed. Better to be safe than sorry. My reciting was soon interrupted by a deep, low growl. Cruzer was letting me know something was here. It turned out to be the mailman. Could this be my package from the Monastery? I certainly hoped so. Nope, it was just a letter from my Aunt Mott, who I hadn't seen in many years. Enclosed were several old pictures of me as a child. I sat and reviewed them, one by one. Yes, *time clouds the memory*, but one of those faded photographs took me back to a day I can never forget.

CHAPTER TWELVE

A bright summer morning, I was six at the time. I can remember the roses blooming on the bush I stood in front of as my Aunt snapped the picture.

"Smile Stephen," she requested.

I was all dressed up in my Sunday clothes, although it was a weekday. No, I will never forget that beautiful sunny day we laid my birth mother to rest. The little boy in the picture wasn't smiling though. He looked lost and alone. It had been taken at my grandmother's house just after the funeral. Everyone in the entire family and many friends came to comfort the bereaved.

I remember the Pastor who conducted the service. "Your Mother is in Heaven with the angels," he tried to explain to me. "God has called her home."

"Well, tell him to send her back," I pleaded. "I need her here!" It was more than my little mind was willing to comprehend. The Pastor's words had not given me comfort. I just couldn't understand why God would do such a mean and selfish thing.

My Father just sat in a chair, staring at nothing. No expression on his face, his eyes lifeless and cold. I did not know the man who stared back at me, although he resembled my Daddy. *He is dead inside,* I remembered thinking. I remember he couldn't even feed himself; he was so stricken with grief. My Grandmother would feed him with a spoon; my Uncle Kent bathed him, combed his hair, and shaved him. He was this way for quite some time. It almost felt as if I lost both parents. Why would God do such a terrible thing? The little boy in the picture just couldn't understand.

"Stephen, I'm home" my wife called down the dark corridor.

"Come in here and take a look at this," I called back. The photo my Aunt sent revealed something I did not remember seeing on that sad, summer morning. There at my feet was a gray cloud of mist. It had been so thick it concealed my penny loafers completely. The mist seemed to cast its own shadow as it floated just a few inches off the ground. At first, I thought it to be some sort of lens flare from the camera. Then I noticed what appeared to be a thin tendril of the mist running up my leg. It seemed to be either reaching for, or emitting from the fingers of my right hand.

Natural born flashed through my mind as I realized what I saw. Was this mist a form of spirit manifestation? I certainly had no other explanation for the photo. Had God answered my plea? Had he sent her back? Was that my Mom in the faded photograph taken forty five years ago? I can't say for sure, but I like to think it was.

"I wonder why she sent you the photos?" Lynn asked. "You haven't heard from her in years."

The letter didn't say. The only reply I could think of was *everything happens for a reason.*

~~~~~~~

I chased down all the items from the list Sister gave me. I now
~~~~~~~

had the white candles, salt, and incense she requested. I was still waiting for the rosaries from the Monks' store. Five to seven business days turned into three weeks and each morning I anxiously awaited the mailman's arrival. I was sure they would show up soon. After all, if you can't trust a Monk, then who can you trust?

I packaged the items I did have and dropped them off at Saint Luke's for Father Jim's blessing. I took the liberty of helping myself to a one liter bottle of holy water from the fountain while I was there. Sister was big on holy water and I thought I might use it to try another experiment. My research demanded it!

Turning on my recorder, I took my usual place at the kitchen table. I earlier poured some of the holy water into a plant sprayer so it could be more easily dispersed. The trap was set.

"Who wants coffee?" I asked of no one.

"We are here," the female voice replied.

"Where are you?" I casually inquired.

"Standing behind," she whispered into the recorder. It sounded like the voice of Carol.

"Are you a…DEMON?" I demanded. Tick…tock…

No reply.

"Get out, bitch!" I shouted Grabbing the spray bottle from the table I quickly spun in my chair and shot several misty bursts of the holy contents into the air.

Cruzer jumped up from his resting place at my feet and bolted out of the kitchen. I house trained him with a spray bottle when he was a puppy. If he messed on the floor, I would spray him with water. The look he gave me was priceless. I quickly rewound and listened for a response.

"That's cold… You're mean!" The voice exclaimed.

"Dear Lord" I said out loud as I realized I had sprayed her.

"Help me," was her pitiful sounding plea.

A sudden feeling of guilt overcame me. All she wanted was my help, I then realized. I can t explain how, other than to say that I just knew. I felt as if I betrayed her. *Help me* had been her request and here I was spraying her with holy water.

"Why are you here? I asked.

"We are not evil," had been her whispered reply.

"Is the shadow man…evil?" I prodded. Upon the playback of the recording, I heard a voice definitely not Carol's. It sounded like the deep, dark, angry voice I recorded in my hallway. Could this be in direct response to my question?

"Fuck you!" was the only reply.

Cruzer acted weirder by the day. He spent a lot of time curled up under my desk. He usually does that when a thunder storm is approaching or if someone yells at him. He woke us in the middle of the night with a chorus of mournful howls.

"Probably hears a siren," I said to my wife. "Damn it, Cruzer," I swore as I reluctantly climbed out of bed to see what his problem might be.

He sat on his haunches on the floor of the den, howling into the darkness. He seemed to be pouring out his heart and soul. Do dogs have souls? I wondered as I opened the front door and stepped out into the cool, midnight air. Whatever had him howling could not have been a siren. The night was dead silent and none of the other mutts in the neighborhood were responding. I noticed the moon was full and wondered if that could be the cause of his odd behavior.

"What is it, boy? I inquired.

A whimper was the only reply, but the look he gave me suggested he surely would tell me if he could. As we stood there in the moonlight, I reflected back on my earlier thought. If dogs do possess a soul could they enter heaven? If there are no dogs in heaven, then how could it be paradise? I wondered. Was Cruzer feeling the presence of the spirits haunting me? Could the shadow man be tormenting him in some dreadful way?

He will kill the dog, Sister advised. I wondered if her terrifying prophecy would come true. Not if I could help it! As we walked back inside the house, I took a little of the holy water and poured it into his water dish. I then poured some on my index finger and traced a cross on his forehead. *Better safe than sorry,* Gabreael's words rang in my head. I was planning to contact the monastery in the morning to inquire why my merchandise hadn't arrived. I would hate to have to leave negative feedback for a Monk, but it had been almost a month now and still no package.

"Come on boy" I said, "let's go back to bed." He did not heed my command, though. He headed straight for my office and curled up under my desk. He was definitely afraid of something. Yes... *Something unseen.*

"It's okay, boy," I assured him as I wrapped myself in a blanket and settled down in my chair. He let out a big yawn as he nestled against my feet. Tick...tock...tick...tock... The mantle clock in the den was the only sound.

~~~~~~~

"God... Where am I?" I wondered in my confusion. I awakened to find myself back in the cemetery. An eerie gray mist seemed to shroud the quiet resting place of the dead. I was standing deep inside the rows of stone. Through the gloom, I could see the giant oak tree that stood sentinel over the interred for almost two hundred years.

Am I dead? I thought to myself. *Or am I just dreaming?* There was no reply. I then noticed I had lost the familiar limp that had been hindering me since my injury occurred. Huh, maybe I am dead, I reasoned. My back wasn't hurting at all and I felt like I was seventeen again. As I approached the tree in the center of the
~~~~~~~

stones, I thought I must be seeing things. I could faintly make out the form of a woman. She just stood there in the mist… Watching me.

She was attired in a long black dress and I could see a heavy dark veil concealing her face. She looked to be from another time… another era. I slowly approached the lone figure, still not sure if she was actually there. She stood by a gravestone, its inscription worn away long, long ago. I thought I could hear her softly weeping. As I walked closer to the mysterious form, I paused, but she raised her hand and beckoned me to come nearer. I then felt the familiar emotions of grief and sadness that must have been emanating from… Her?

I've never been able to handle the emotions of grief very well and I wondered what I might do to comfort her. Would I even know what to say?

"I am deeply sorry for your loss, ma'am," I quietly stated.

"Stephen," she whispered. "You must help me."

I slowly drew near to her, wondering how in the hell she knew my name. "Do I know you… Miss?" I hesitantly inquired.

"I've been waiting," she sighed.

"Waiting for whom?" I asked her.

"Don't you remember me… Stephen?" She replied in that same whispered tone.

"No," I answered. "I'm afraid I don't." This wasn't a lie as I didn't remember her and I was definitely afraid.

"I'm not dead," she enlightened me in a tone that sounded more urgent, more desperate than before.

No shit! Sherlock, I thought. "Why are you here alone?" I inquired.

She did not immediately answer. "I don't know," she finally whispered, apparently as confused as I now was.

"How can I help you?" I asked her, still wondering where she might know me from.

"Pray for me," she whispered.

I reflected back on that first EVP I recorded there on my initial visit. "I am not a priest," I told her. "I really don't feel qualified."

No reply.

"Would you like me to take you to the church office, ma'am?" I thought maybe the young Pastor's words might comfort her. Even though I wasn't looking forward to seeing him again, I just couldn't leave her out there alone… Weeping in the graveyard. I gently took hold of her arm.

"Release me," she pleaded.

"Okay, I'm sorry," I said as I immediately let her go and took a couple of steps back. "Let me go get the Pastor," I offered, as I suddenly felt the urge to get away from her. She was creeping me out. She must be crazy, I thought… Or maybe I was.

"Give me the *power*!" she suddenly demanded.

"Excuse me, what did you say?" I thought I heard what she said, but I wanted to be sure.

No reply.

"I don't know how," I told her that wasn't a lie either.

"Well then, why are *you* here, Stephen?" she inquired.

That seemed a rather odd question. Yes, rather odd, indeed. "I talk to… The dead..." I hesitantly confided. "They…. Haunt me," I told her in a whisper as I glanced around to be sure no one could overhear my confession.

"Don't you remember me, Stephen?" She again asked as she took a step closer.

"No," I again insisted.

"Yes, they seek your *power*… Spirit man," she hissed.

"Spirit man?" I repeated her words. How could she know that?

"We are not all…evil." she replied.

Damn, I must be dreaming. I sure hoped I was. "Carol…? Is that you?" I nervously asked, as my mind struggled to make sense of what my eyes and ears were telling it. The voice did sound vaguely familiar to me.

"Look," she whispered as she pointed her glove-clad finger toward the ground.

There lying at my feet I saw the softball I searched for on that hot evening so long ago. It came slowly rolling out of the mist. I stood staring down at it in disbelief. "Do you remember me now, Stephen?"

A familiar feeling slowly began to creep over me. "Maybe I should be going now," I told her, still wondering where that ball had been for the past thirty-three years.

"My ship awaits us," the voice then whispered in a decidedly less feminine tone.

I looked back up at the shrouded figure, to see she was slowly lifting her veil. "Oh, God, no," I whimpered.

"God is not with you now," she chuckled in a cracked voice.

My eyes widened as I witnessed the horror now standing before me. With the veil removed, I could indeed recognize the face underneath. It was old Mr. Foard. His eyes were lifeless and cold. They stared back at me in the gloom. His mouth was open in that same silent scream. I didn't plan to wait around for the insects to crawl out this time, however. Nope... I didn't wish to ever see that again.

"Natural causes," he whispered. "Yes, natural, indeed."

"Holy shit!" I screamed. "Get away from me… Please!"

"Run, Steve… Run," he taunted in a much deeper voice.

I heard the voice taunt again as I realized I could not move. I tried to run, but nothing was happening. My limbs simply refused to obey the adrenaline laced impulses from my brain. I stood there frozen, mortified, as I watched the cross-dressing cadaver come ever closer, our eyes still locked in that unearthly gaze.

The stench of death reeked on his breath as he leaned in close and whispered into my ear. "Meow… Has curiosity killed the cat?"

I tried to back away from him, but only managed to fall against a headstone.

"Knowledge can be… Painful," he whispered in a cackling voice, his mouth drawn into an evil grin. His black tongue writhed with what appeared to be small maggots as he continued to enlighten me.

God, I hope I am dreaming this shit. The haunting vision of my wife standing in my doorway with that dead look in her eyes filled my mind.

"Seek and ye shall find," the rotting corpse assured me, his putrid breath causing me to gag.

It was again my turn to scream. I suddenly snapped awake in my chair. Cruzer let out a yelp as I kicked him in my effort to rise and flee. I still could not run however and fell flat on my face. The blanket around my legs tripped me up. I lay in the darkness, gasping for air, still not exactly sure of where I was. Gradually my breathing started to return to normal. Electric jolts of pain shot up and down my spine, my hair was damp with sweat.

I must have had a bad dream, I thought. *God, I hoped it was just a dream.*

"Stephen?" There was that voice again. "Stephen, are you all right? I heard you call out in your sleep. What are you doing on the floor?" Lynn asked as she switched on the light.

"I must have had a nightmare," I answered, still not sure if it was just a dream.

"Well, come on to bed!" she commanded. "I have to get up and go to work in the morning."

"No, you go ahead," I told her. There would be no more sleep for me tonight. I slowly rose and climbed back into my chair. I needed a smoke. I tried to light a cigarette, but my hands shook so badly that the matches kept going out. "Son of a bitch, what the hell was that all about?" I muttered to no one.

Cruzer went and curled up in bed with Lynn. After his rude awakening, I couldn't blame him. I kicked him good. I wondered what could have caused me to wake up on the floor, gasping for breath in a cold sweat. What could it all mean? Was this just a stress induced nightmare? Or could it have been caused by something else? I wasn't sure, but whatever the cause I was certain I didn't want to go there again. I picked up the bottle of holy water from my desk and dabbed a little on my index finger. I then made the sign of the cross on my own forehead. *Better to be safe than sorry,* Gabreael's words again rang in my ears.

CHAPTER THIRTEEN

The next morning, I shot a quick email to the Monastery asking when I might expect to receive my blessed package. If it didn't show up soon, I would have to proceed without the rosaries.

Sister phoned and asked how things were going here at home. I assured her I was reading the verses she prescribed morning, noon, and night. I also related the terrifying nightmare I couldn't quite remember, that still had me shaken and dreading the thought of ever sleeping again.

"It was a warning," she stated.

"A warning?" I questioned.

"It was a warning from God that you should not attempt to communicate with the demonic," she went on with her interpretation of my living nightmare.

"I have never attempted to communicate with demons," I assured her. "I was just conducting my research."

"They are seeking to destroy you, Stephen" she promised. "God is warning you to stop this blasphemous behavior."

Yes, the dream may have indeed been a warning, but I didn't think God had anything to do with it.

"Do you want that demon to molest your wife?" she inquired.

"Hell no!" I responded. I didn't even realize demon molestation was a possibility.

"Have her anoint her orifices with the holy water," Sister instructed.

"Ah come on, Sister. That is the most ludicrous sounding thing I ever heard."

"You must do exactly as I say, Stephen," she admonished me. "Morning, noon, and night!"

I just couldn't imagine how I might relay her bizarre instructions to Lynn. I ended our conversation with a promise that I would not record, or speak to them, again.

~~~~~~~

The Monk's reply to my email read:

> *Sorry for the delay. We ran out of pet medals and it took a few days for us to restock them. The rosaries were mailed three weeks ago. Please pardon any inconvenience that this may have caused.*
>
> *May God bless you!*

"Damn it!" I swore. *Just my luck!* The rosaries had apparently been lost in the mail. "Leave it to the government to screw everything up," I complained to no one.

I replied to the email, stating neither package arrived and that I needed them in the worst way. If the demonic presence here could be ousted by religious provocation, then I wanted all of the back up
~~~~~~~

I could get. Sister was convinced I was dealing with pure evil and after all, evil was her specialty.

The Monk replied almost immediately stating that even though I hadn't purchased insurance for my shipment, he would reship my order as soon as possible.

Father Jim's secretary also called to inform me my blessed salt, candles, and incense were ready and could be picked up at the church office. I jumped into my truck and sped to the church, wanting to have the items in my possession in case something unseen chose to make its presence known. I asked if Father Jim might be available. I wanted to fill him in on the things Lynn and I experienced since we last spoke.

"Father Jim is in the cathedral," she advised me. "You will find him in the confessional."

I thanked her, then tucked the package under my arm and headed for the confession booth. The cathedral was empty of parishioners except for the little old lady who was exiting the right side of the booth. She smiled and nodded at me as we passed.

Her confession must have went well, I thought, as I took a deep breath and opened the door to the small chamber hoping that mine would also turn out well. It was almost completely dark inside, but I could make out the silhouette of Father Jim's kindly face. A wall separated us and communication was conducted through a veiled window.

"Forgive me, Father, for I have sinned," I nervously stated. I had never been to confession before and wondered exactly what I should say. Heck, I wasn't even of that faith.

"What do you wish to confess, my son?" the voice asked through the veil.

"It is me, Father… Stephen. I wish to confess my sins."

"Continue, my son."

"I will not bother to list them, Father… God already knows what they are. I just want to ask Him to forgive me."

There was no immediate reply. "He already has, my son," he finally answered.

"Pray for me, Father," I then requested. "I am a man in search of my religion." I was sincere in wanting his help to cleanse *my* soul.

He offered a prayer for my salvation and then added one for protection for good measure.

I then went on to confide in him as to another burden I carried. "I have been reading the Bible a lot lately, Father," I confided. "There is one verse in there that has me really concerned."

"And which verse is that, my son?" he inquired.

"Do not turn to mediums or psychics; do not seek them out to be defiled by them. I am the LORD your God." I quoted the scripture from Leviticus 19.

"You did not seek her out," he thoughtfully replied. "You said you were not aware she was a medium when you first contacted her for help."

"No, but that's not what bothers me, Father."

"Then what is it, my son?"

"I'm psychic," I reminded him. We ended my impromptu visit with his assurance that God had indeed forgiven me. I certainly hoped He had.

"Always remember, Stephen. God is with you," Father Jim assured me. I didn't feel worthy, but I had certainly hoped He was.

~~~~~~~

"The Lord is my shepherd, I shall not want," I read from the list of verses Sister had given me. "Thy rod and Thy staff, they comfort me." Somehow the words made me feel not so alone. My blessing from Father Jim gave me courage. Courage to do what I felt must
~~~~~~~

be done. I lit the blessed incense and then the candles, placing them on the dresser in our bedroom. I continued with the reading of the verses as I dipped my finger in the bottle of holy water and made the sign of the cross on both windows and the bedroom doorway. I then took the blessed salt and laid out a thin line on the window sills and the top of the door frame.

"I am a child of God," I proclaimed to any evil presence that might have been listening. "This is my house, this is my castle, and I am taking back what is mine. If you are not of Heaven, then you are not welcome here. I command you to leave here, NOW!"

I continued this ritual in every room in my small abode hoping to banish any negative spirits lurking within. I didn't really know what I was doing, but I couldn't let things go on as they had for the past six weeks. Gabreael's words flashed through my mind. *Human spirits are of free will and cannot be ousted by religious provocation,* she advised.

It wasn't human spirits I feared as they were apparently here for my help. Whether the young Pastor believed in demons or not, the spirits in my home certainly seemed to. *Fear the Demons* had been their message from the cemetery and something told me they were speaking from experience.

I suddenly realized perhaps I was doing this as much for them as I was for Lynn and myself. Maybe this was the help they so desperately sought. A place safe from whatever dark forces tormented their lost souls. Could this be why they followed me home in the first place? Or had the Nun been right? *They are all demonic*, she said.

I finished my improvised cleansing ritual in every room of the house. I expected some sort of response or maybe the shadow man would show himself and challenge me. Much to my relief, however, this was not the case. I didn't hear or see anything out of the ordinary other than myself in the mirror, a tired looking old man with a candle in one hand and a Bible in the other.

Cruzer followed me around the house as if trying to figure out just what was going on. Had his Master finally gone crazy? Shouting Bible verses and spraying holy water everywhere, all by candle light? The look he gave me seemed to confirm my intuitions. *They will kill the dog,* Sister warned. The pet medal still hadn't shown up, nor had my rosaries. I felt as if I could have used them on that night, but this just couldn't wait any longer. I gave the dog a blast from the spray bottle, which sent him bolting down the hallway and behind the couch in the den.

Better safe than sorry, Gabreael's words again rang in my head. *Maybe my cleansing hadn't worked*, I thought. Maybe my faith just wasn't strong enough. Tick…tock... Self doubt slowly started to ease its way into my mind, pushing my newly found courage aside. I suddenly wished Lynn was home so I wouldn't feel so alone. She had to work late again and I felt very lonely, because with the self doubt came fear. Tick…tock... I just stood there silent… Listening. Tick…tock... The mantle clock in the den was the only sound. Tick…tock... The air in the house did seem a bit lighter, though.

I began to think, maybe, my efforts hadn't been in vain. Tick… tock…

Tap…

What the hell? Tick… tock… Cruzer emitted the same low growl as on that evening in the hallway, except this time he stayed hidden behind the sofa. He didn't want to get sprayed again. Tick… tock….

Tap...

There it was again. Tick…tock... But where was it coming from? Tick…tock… I stood there motionless, frozen. Tick…tock… My ears strained to hear the slightest sound. Tick…tock…

TAP....

It was coming from overhead... The attic? I stood silently listening for the next five minutes or so. Tick...tock... The mantle clock in the den was the only sound. It slowly started to dawn on me what I just heard.

Three taps or knocks as in *give us a sign of your presence*. The same response Joe asked for on that afternoon which now seemed eons ago. The same three taps I heard on the night I pursued the shadow man down the hallway. Or could they have been footsteps? Then another thought occurred to me, one I should have thought of sooner. I had just blessed the entire house—except for the attic! Just then I heard another low growl from behind the sofa. Cruzer was letting me know something was here.

Yes... *Something unseen...* But not unheard. Yes, it tapped three times, that I was sure of. But now I was hearing something that sent my skin creeping up my aching back. A soft, low growling could faintly be heard. I slowly realized this time it wasn't the dog. It came from somewhere above me. It was coming from the attic.

CHAPTER FOURTEEN

The attic access door is located in the ceiling of our bedroom closet. I stood at the bottom of the wooden ladder that led up to the small hatchway wondering if I should even attempt to climb it without Lynn being there to assist me. What if I lost my balance and fell? Dr. Ashe would not have approved, I was sure. The last thing I needed was to fall and further injure my spine. That would require another surgery and God knows I feared that. I just spent the last nine months trying to recover from the last one.

No one had been up there in a long time. Probably not since last Christmas, and then only to retrieve the large boxes of decorations stored up there.

"Leave here now!" I commanded from the doorway of the closet, trying my best not to let the fear in my voice betray me. "Don't make me come up there!" I shouted.

No reply.

Then another thought crept into my muddled mind. What if I

get up there and something bad happens? What if I can't get back down? The small ladder was built onto the wall and although it was only eight feet high, it was straight up. I took the bottle of holy water and made the sign of the cross on my forehead. *Better safe than sorry.*

I tucked the Bible under one arm and stepped up on the first rung. I was forced to leave the still flickering candles and the incense on the night stand. There was no way I could climb up there with them, so I would have to leave them behind. *Maybe I should just wait. At least, until Lynn gets home. No,* I reasoned, *I brought this thing here and it is up to me to be rid of it.* I really didn't want to subject her to anymore than I already had. I hoisted myself up to the second rung, my back already feeling the strain. I carefully made my way up one step at a time, clinging to the ladder like my life depended on it.

Finally, I reached the hatchway and with my free hand gave it an upward shove. It wouldn't budge. *What the hell?* I pushed upwards again. The Bible slipped from under my other arm and fell to the floor of the closet "Crap," I muttered under my breath. *Just my luck!* I stepped up another rung and, trying to use my legs instead of my back, I placed my shoulder against the hatchway then pushed up with all the strength I could muster. There was a loud crash as the hatchway flew open. I could hear the sound of glass shattering.

What in the hell was that? I slowly peeked my head thru the hatchway, still not sure if I should go up any further. I felt for the string I knew hung above me to turn on the lone light bulb and chase the darkness away. Finding it, I gave a tug with my free hand. *Click*, nothing. I pulled the string again; *click,* but still no light. "Shit," I muttered. This wasn't turning out as I planned.

Cautiously, I hoisted myself up through the hatch and onto the attic floor, now wishing I had thought to bring a flashlight up with me. I couldn't even see my hand in front of my face. I slowly got to my feet, panting from the effort it took to force open the hatch and pull myself through.

I stood there for a moment just listening, wincing from the twinges of pain shooting up and down my spine. Fishing my lighter from my pocket, I was able to have at least some light to see by. Although it wasn't much light, it was a whole lot better than none. Kneeling down I discovered what had caused the loud crash. A large box of Christmas decorations was over turned and spilled out onto the floor. I could see the brightly colored fragments of glass glinting in the flickering flame of my Bic.

It had to have been on top of the hatch, but how could it have gotten there? I wondered. Someone or *something* placed it there, I reasoned. Apparently, whatever was up here didn't wish to be discovered. Had my cleansing ritual been working after all? Had my blessing of the downstairs forced this thing to take refuge in the attic? Was it afraid of me and my blessed incense and candles? Had the reading of the scripture caused it to run and hide?

"Get out of my house, you bastard, this ends here and now. Do not think I'm afraid of you, for I will hunt you down!" I shouted, sure I had it on the run. "God stands with me," I proclaimed. "You have no power here."

Thump, thump, thump.

What the hell? Footsteps? I could then hear another low growl emitting from the other end of the attic. It was answered by another coming from downstairs. Cruzer must have heard it and was challenging whatever this was only a few feet away from me now. I reached down and retrieved the spray bottle of holy water hooked on my belt as I listened to the footsteps draw closer to the hatchway.

Thump, thump, thump.

"Get thee behind me, Satan," I recited the words Jesus commanded as he carried the cross up the mountain to his death, sincerely hoping these words would not proceed my own. It was then I felt a hot breath on the back of my neck.

"Power..." the dark voice whispered into my ear.

I quickly spun around, dropping my lighter, it startled me so badly. If I was afraid before, it was nothing compared to now. Trembling there, alone in the dark, I was certain I was now standing face to face with whatever this—*Thing*—was.

Suddenly, I was pushed backwards by what felt like an index finger which violently poked my right shoulder. It was accompanied by a loud pop that reminded me of the sound of static electricity.

I screamed in terror as I realized how strong this entity actually was and that I was alone and face to face with it up here in the dark. I reached out for something to hold onto. I managed to grab a rafter with my free hand. I raised the spray bottle and blasted the contents into the darkness.

It let out a tormented growl as if it were in pain. I aimed in the direction of the sound and sprayed another stream of the blessed liquid.

"Dear God, save me," I prayed. I then felt a rush of air sweep past me and could hear the screen of the eave vent whistling as if some great gust of wind passed through it. The vacuum created by its departing caused the hatchway door to slam back down. I let out a startled little yelp at the sound of it slamming. Then there was silence. I faintly heard the patter of rain drops begin to fall on the roof. I stood there for several minutes, just listening for the slightest sound, the slightest breath, the faintest footstep. The beating of my heart was the only sound.

I slowly made my way back down the ladder, afraid to put too much trust in my still trembling legs. I reached up and pulled the hatch closed with my free hand, taking the time to spray the sign of the cross on the door. My back screamed in protest as I bent down to retrieve my Bible from the floor of the closet. I limped into the bathroom, flipped on the lights and stood in front of the mirror.

The old man who stared back at me looked like he had been through hell. I could see it in those haunted, brown eyes and hear it in those rasping breaths. Pulling back my shirt collar, I could see a faint red mark where I had been poked by the invisible force. There was now an aching in my shoulder, way down deep inside. It still plagues me to this day.

~~~~~~~

Doctor Ashe would later diagnose the cause as arthritis, but I know differently. It has cost me many a sleepless night, my waking up and hurting so bad I couldn't get back to sleep. Even the sleeping pills didn't seem to phase it. Yes, knowledge can indeed be painful, this I now know for a fact. The air in the house seemed lighter, though. I felt as if whatever dark presence had been here was gone. Had my do it yourself banishment actually worked? I wasn't sure, but I couldn't help but pray it had.

I spent the next few months buried deep in my research. I was spending countless hours online and at the local library reading everything I could find on the subject of the afterlife and the paranormal. I hadn't tried to record anymore since the house blessing as Sister advised against it. She said it would only encourage the demon to return and to let the pain in my shoulder serve as a reminder.
~~~~~~~

CHAPTER FIFTEEN

Gabreael called to check on me from time to time. She also advised me to stop my communication with any human spirits that may still linger here, as recording them just gives them encouragement to make themselves known. So I took her advice and didn't record or return to the cemetery.

I knew the Turners were still around, though. Occasionally, I would hear them softly talking in another room. I didn't acknowledge their presence, though, as bad as I wanted to talk to them. They seemed to like to play little jokes on me at times. Nothing scary, nothing of ill intent, just little jokes which I think they found very amusing.

Carol liked to wait until I was undressed and stepping into the shower. Then she would say my name so I would think Lynn was calling me from outside the bathroom door. The first couple of times this happened, I cut the shower off and answered, thinking it was, in fact, my wife's voice. Pretty soon I caught on and just pretended like I didn't hear her.

The little boy seemed to like to hide things from me. I would find these items in the oddest of places. The first thing I reach for each morning is my glasses. I can't even see the time on the alarm clock without them. I keep them on my nightstand, right beside the bed. Sometimes they will be gone. They usually turn up somewhere under the bed or maybe on the dresser. The problem is I can't see well enough to find them. I could just imagine the grin on his young face as he watched the sleepy headed, squinting old man crawl around under the bed searching for them.

I told Gabreael about these odd occurrences when she called, but I didn't mention them to Sister. She would have me shouting scripture verses again. Morning, noon, and night!

I felt as if I had a choice to make now, though, and it was one I couldn't avoid any longer. Now that I knew about my sixth sense, should I just ignore it? Or should I continue my research and explore it? My life was forever changed because of my research. Things would never be as they were before all of this began—at least not through my eyes.

I would let God decide. I would ask Him for His guidance. I would ask Him…for a sign. I said a silent prayer then, wondering what kind of reply I might receive.

Dear God, if I do possess a gift, if it was given to me for some purpose, if I am following the correct path, please show me, Lord. Amen.

Little did I know then I wouldn't have long to wait. They say the Lord works in mysterious ways and I now would have to agree. Two things happened to me the very next day I cannot explain in any other way.

~~~~~~~

The first sign came at our local park attending a festival. Our
~~~~~~~

little town has a festival every year to commemorate the day it was founded. It was one of those sunny spring mornings that made you glad to be outdoors. I usually avoid those festivals each year as I have never liked large crowds, but on this day Lynn had to work and I decided to check it out on a whim. As I wandered through the maze of kiddy rides, hot dog vendors, and clowns, I was reminded of the old county fairs of my youth.

I noticed a crowd of folks gathering in front of the large bandstand that stood way down at the other end of the park. I decided to meander over and check out the brass band. I could hear them warming up and besides the exercise would do me good. As I made my way through the crowd, a man and a teenage boy approached me. The boy looked to be about thirteen or so. I noticed the man held the boy's hand.

"Excuse me, sir," the gentleman said to me. "I am sorry to bother you, but my son has something he would like to give you," he explained.

"And what might that be?" I asked as I wondered what it could possibly be. I had never seen these people before. I didn't know them.

"He wants to give you a hug," the man told me.

"Okay," I replied, although I still couldn't imagine why.

The man let go of the teenager's hand and the boy grabbed me and gave me a bear hug. He squeezed me with all his strength and would not let go.

"Marty… Stop! Let him go now. Please excuse him, sir," the man pleaded as he pulled the boy from me. "I've never seen him act this way before," he said in an astounded tone of voice. "I'm sorry, please excuse him," he again pleaded.

I assured the man it was all right. The boy had not hurt me.

"It is the weirdest thing," the man then said. "I don't know what's gotten into him."

I could hear the tone of relief in his voice as he realized I wasn't injured or upset by his son's actions.

"We were leaving the festival when Marty started trying to tell me something," he explained. "He started pulling me back towards the park." He went on to inform me, "When I asked him what he wanted he just said… Hugs, and then pulled me through the crowd and straight to you."

I noticed he had taken the boy's hand again.

"Marty is autistic," he told me. "I'm sorry, I don't know what's gotten into him," he repeated as he shook his head and led the boy back towards the parking lot.

I watched them walk away into the crowd.

The boy turned one last time to look back at me and smile as his father led him on.

I stood there for the next few minutes enjoying the music and wondering if this could possibly be the sign I asked for. I decided to ask for further validation. I then said another short silent prayer.

Father, if you sent the boy to me as a sign, thank you. If so, please acknowledge it with another. I need to know for sure. Amen.

Blacksnake, I heard the voice ring in my head. It sounded like my own voice, but I knew I didn't say it. It is hard for me to explain, but it wasn't a thought either. Not one that made any sense. I heard the voice on my way home from the festival, just as I turned onto my street.

Blacksnake? Could I have just imagined it? No, I didn't think so. It was too loud… Too clear. It just didn't make any sense to me. *Blacksnake?* This was not a conscious thought on my part. I was sure of that. I drove up the hill and turned into my drive, still wondering why that word sounded in my head. Had I actually heard it audibly through my ears? I didn't think so. What could it mean?

I climbed out of my truck and limped down the sidewalk, still deep in thought about what I just experienced. I fumbled the house keys as I was inserting it into the lock and swore as I watched them fall to the concrete. My back ached and I really needed to get to the bathroom. “Shit,” I complained to no one. “Just my luck.”

As I slowly bent down to pick them up, I saw something that caused me to jump back and almost wet myself. There on my front porch, lying stretched out in the shade not two feet from where my hand had just been, was a five foot long monster of a snake. Yes, a Blacksnake! I stood there with my mouth hanging open for several minutes.

This was surely the sign I prayed for less than an hour ago. I tapped my foot on the concrete and the snake raised his head slightly, testing the air with his rapidly flicking tongue. “Go now,” I softly spoke to it, “your work here is done.” The snake slowly turned and slithered off the porch as if he understood my words. I bent down and retrieved my keys.

“Thank you, Father,” I softly said. “Now I know for sure.”

~~~~~~~

I couldn’t wait to tell Gabreael what just happened. I wanted to share my validation which I was convinced had been heaven sent. I felt so uplifted, so encouraged to continue my research. After all, communicating with spirits was my specialty—albeit a bizarre one.

Now I just needed to figure out my higher purpose. I now knew I was chosen to receive this talent for a reason. I just wasn’t sure what it might be. Maybe Gabreael could shed some light on this mystery. I gave her a call and in my excitement didn’t even let her get hello out of her mouth. So she listened patiently as I related the events as they had just occurred. I told her I was convinced I was meant to continue my research, not to prove their existence, but to somehow help them.
~~~~~~~

"I will be in Asheville in a week," she informed me. She said she had a private investigation she had been contacted on. "Would you like to come and assist me?" she asked.

"Me," I questioned her.

"Yes," she replied. "If you want to help, you can come and help me."

"What should I bring?" I inquired.

"Just yourself, a change of clothes, a camera, and a tape recorder," she answered. "Plan to be up all night."

We ended the conversation with her promise to email me the address of the house we would be investigating. I was elated at the invitation. I really felt honored she would think enough of me to ask me for my help. I just hoped I wouldn't let her down. I was happy to have something to look forward to. However, I was a little apprehensive as well.

~~~~~~~

Could I actually help someone else who had been experiencing the same type of activity Lynn and I endured? I certainly hoped I could. The one thing I wasn't prepared to do was leave this family as MAPS left me, afraid and alone. I felt as if I owed Gabreael. She was the only one who believed me and now in me. For that, I will be forever indebted.

"Does anybody want coffee" I asked as I sat at the kitchen table, my recorder in hand. I hadn't tried to communicate with the spirits in my house in months and I wasn't sure they would even answer me. I wanted to see if Carol or Andy would talk to me as they did in the past. "Is anybody with me now?" I continued with my questions. I waited a few seconds and then rewound the recorder.

"Yes, coffee," the female voice faintly whispered in reply.

Upon hearing this, I immediately hit record again. "Carol, is
~~~~~~~

that you?"

"Yes… Carol," came the whisper upon playback.

"Carol, why are you here?" I asked her the question I most wanted an answer to. I knew they followed me from the cemetery, I just didn't know exactly why.

"Will you…help us?"

"Yes, Carol, I want to help you. I just don't know how," I answered. "How can I help you Carol?" I inquired.

"Cross us," she whispered into the microphone.

"Tell me how!" I shouted in my frustration.

She answered with just one word. "Light..." she whispered.

"What light?"

There was no reply. The conversation was apparently over. Either she didn't know what to say or maybe ran out of the energy needed to say it. I certainly felt drained of energy recently. I thought back on that night in the attic.

Power, the phantom voice whispered just before it poked me. Was it drawing energy from me? Or was it giving me a little taste of its own. Just another question to ponder, I thought to myself as I rubbed my stiff shoulder. I had been having dreams about that evening as well. Dreams I can't ever seem to remember upon awakening. But on those nights, I would set up in bed covered in sweat, my shoulder throbbing, my ears strained to hear the slightest sound. Tick…tock…tick…tock...

CHAPTER SIXTEEN

Ding-dong…

I could hear the chime sound as I pressed the lighted button. The house was a large structure and didn't look to be old at all. Nice neighborhood, I thought as I waited for someone to come to the door. I was greeted by a young girl. She looked to be around thirteen or so. She smiled revealing her braces and introduced herself as Amy.

"My name is Stephen. I believe I'm expected," I informed her, returning the smile.

Amy led me into the large foyer. The vaulted ceiling reminded me of a cathedral.

"Please have a seat," she invited, as she led me into the den. "The others are upstairs. I will tell them you're here."

I sat there nervously as I waited for Gabreael to come down and meet me for the first time in person. In a few moments I heard footsteps descending the wooden staircase. I looked up to see the only person in the world, other than my wife, who didn't think I was crazy. I stood and we introduced ourselves, giving each other the once over as we shook hands.

I had expected a hug from her after we talked so many hours on the telephone and by email. But I realized she needed to keep this professional. After all, we were here to investigate a haunting and try to help someone. Someone who maybe questioned their own sanity, changed their own religious beliefs, and now wondered who to turn to.

Gabreael then led me upstairs. "I want you to tell me if you feel anything," she instructed. We had been met at the top of the stairs by Amelia, the client, and Athena, who also was there to assist Gabreael. Gabreael introduced me and then asked them to wait for us downstairs. She then gave me a tour of the entire upper floor. We walked slowly through each room, taking the time to stop for a minute in each one.

I really didn't see or feel anything out of the ordinary. It was just a very nice, extravagantly furnished home.

"We just have a couple of rooms left and then we will join the others downstairs." She led me across the hallway and into what had to be, the daughter's bedroom.

~~~~~~~

The room held a large, four-post bed that took up almost half of the room. By the way it was decorated, I knew it belonged to the young girl. As we entered, I suddenly did feel something different about this room. The air had a familiar heaviness to it. It felt... thicker... harder to breath. The hair rose up on my arms and I could feel a slight tingle run down my spine.

"This is the room, Gabreael," I quietly said.

"What do you feel?" she asked in reply.

"Heaviness in my chest... The air is thicker here," I answered.
~~~~~~~

"Good," she said. "Very good."

I felt as if I passed a test. I somehow felt validated.

The client's claims of activity sounded rather familiar to me. Footsteps, feelings of being watched, and whispering voices were the experiences Amelia recounted. The young girl just sat there nodding her head as her mother recounted the occurrences that had taken place in the house recently. Amelia went on to tell us of the previous owners of the place. They had been an elderly couple who had the house custom built for themselves and their adult daughter, Beverly.

Beverly had been born with Downs Syndrome and required constant care and supervision. Her life sadly came to an end in her thirty-fifth year. She died in the home due to complications resulting from her condition.

Amelia went onto to inform us the previous owners stated the reason for selling the home as grief. There were just too many memories of their beloved daughter in the home for them to remain there.

"Do you know which room the girl died in?" I interrupted. Then suddenly I feared I was speaking out of turn. Gabreael was the one conducting the client interview, not me. "I'm sorry, please continue," I sheepishly said.

"Yes," Amy excitedly interjected. "In my room!" she exclaimed as she nervously glanced at her mother for approval. "She died in my room," she repeated. "In my bed," she went on.

"In your bed?" I asked her as I didn't immediately comprehend what she said.

"Yes," the young girl informed me. "She died in my bedroom, in the four poster bed. All of my bedroom furniture once belonged to Beverly."

Amelia went on to inform us that most all of the furniture in the house belonged to the previous owners. "They just said they had no use for all of it and it was included in the price of the house," she went on to explain.

Gabreael continued with the questions as Athena took notes. "Have you or anyone in your family ever used an Ouija board?" she asked Amelia.

"Oh… Well, no," she replied.

I could hear the hesitation in Amelia's voice and noticed the expression on her face as she answered.

Gabreael seemed not to have noticed and continued with her questions. Suddenly, I heard a noise that sounded like it came from somewhere upstairs. It sounded like a heavy step or maybe a stomp on the hard wood floor.

"Listen!" I said.

Everyone went quiet.

"Did anyone else just hear that?" I questioned.

"I thought I heard something too," Amy answered.

So there we sat, our senses alert, our ears strained to hear the slightest sound.

"It was probably just the house settling." Gabreael barely got the words out of her mouth when it sounded again.

Thump.

Everyone seemed to hear it then. I glanced at Amy, noting the expression on her young face. I had seen that look before. It was one of genuine fear.

Thump.

We all heard the noise again.

"I don't think that noise is from the house settling," I said.

"That sounded like someone stomping their foot on the floor," Athena then remarked.

"Like a child who hasn't gotten its way," Gabreael added.

"Steve, come with me," she instructed.

We ascended the stairs, stopping to listen as we reached the upper floor. Everything was silent. We then slowly crept toward the girl's room trying our best to be stealthy in our movements. As we made our way down the dimly lit corridor, we could see the door to Amy's room was now closed.

That door was open when we went downstairs, I was sure of it.

Gabreael reached into her shoulder bag and pulled out a digital camera. Using sign language, she instructed me to ready mine.

I extracted my camera from its case fastened to my belt and turned it on. We slowly crept closer to the closed door of the bedroom. We stopped when we reached the doorway and just listened for a moment. The house was completely silent. The beating of our hearts was the only sound.

"Ready?" Gabreael whispered the question.

I nodded my head in reply.

"On three," she then whispered. "One… Two… Three! She swung the door open and we entered the room single file, snapping off pictures in every direction, our camera flashes eerily illuminating the room.

"Steve, did you feel that?" she asked me, as I indeed felt a cool breeze lift the hair on my arm. "Its running from us… Follow me," she instructed. She quickly walked back into the hallway, snapping photos as she went.

I remained in the room just long enough to pop off a couple more shots, and then followed her down the hallway.

"This way," she advised as I followed her into the large bedroom at the end of the hall.

We entered the room with our cameras blazing. We must have taken fifty or more photos in the two minutes we were there. I noticed Gabreael stopped taking photos and was reviewing on the camera display screen.

"I think we may have caught something," she informed me.

I looked over her shoulder at the small screen and noticed what looked to be a blurry mist on the picture.

"Let's go back downstairs," she suggested. "We can review the pictures on my laptop.

"Wait, Gabreael," I whispered.

"What is it?" she asked.

"Amelia is lying to us… I'm pretty sure," I told her. I then explained the wavering tone I detected in her voice when Gabreael asked her about the Ouija board.

"Time will tell," was her only reply.

~~~~~~~

Making our way downstairs, we crowded around Gabriel's laptop computer as she loaded our camera cards into the machine. We reviewed the pictures, one by one, as we sipped fresh coffee which Amelia brought to us on a silver tray. She was a very gracious hostess I remember thinking at the time.

The photos from Amy's bedroom did not reveal anything but a couple of large orbs. Gabreael explained they were probably just dust particles caught in the flash of the camera.

I wasn't so sure they were just dust, though. I had seen this type of anomaly before, except mine was in broad daylight in the cemetery and on film. The perfectly round ball of light on her screen seemed to swirl with energy as she zoomed in on it.

"Dust particles, my ass," I unintentionally blurted. *Crap… did I just say that out loud?*

Gabreael gave me a look that spoke volumes to me. Although it was just a quick glance, I knew exactly what she was telling me. *Don't dispute what I say, let me do the talking*. After all, it was her case, not mine. Finally we got around to the pictures we took in the
~~~~~~~

end bedroom.

There, on one of the photos, was a blurry, white mist. It seemed to be in motion when the shutter snapped. It was rather large in size and I judged it to be around four feet in height.

"What in the world could that be?" Amelia asked as she tried to comprehend what she was seeing.

I could hear the fear in her voice as she asked the question.

Gabreael explained to her it could have been caused by a reflection from the camera flash bouncing off a mirror.

Camera flash, my ass, I thought to myself. I had seen a mist similar to this one before, except it was in a faded photograph taken in broad daylight forty-five years ago.

"Well, that's all the photos," Gabreael then said and turned off the laptop. "I will review them closer when I get back home tomorrow."

Amelia and Amy then excused themselves for the evening. They decided to turn in as it was already after midnight.

"I hope they can help us," I heard Amy say to her mother as they were walking down the hallway to the master bedroom located on the first floor of the house. "I'm tired of not being able to sleep upstairs in my room."

~~~~~~~

"Do you know what this is?" Gabreael asked as she handed me an EMF meter.

"Yes, I've seen one of those before," I assured her. Handing Athena a temperature gun, she instructed us to measure and record baseline readings of electromagnetic field and ambient air temperature in each room of the house. Gabreael wanted to review our photos again on her laptop, now that the client wasn't there looking over her shoulder.

Athena and I decided to start in the basement and work our way
~~~~~~~

up. We took readings in each section and room of the large cellar and recorded them on a pad as we went. Athena was a very intelligent young lady. She must have been around thirty-five or so. She had a very pleasant energy around her and we hit it off almost immediately.

"I am so happy to get to work with you, Stephen," she said. "Gabreael said you are extremely gifted."

I felt embarrassed, but flattered by the compliment. "Time will tell," was my only reply.

We continued our sweeps in every room of the house, except of course the master bedroom where Amelia and Amy were now sleeping. We reported back to Gabreael that our baseline readings were all recorded. No phantom cold spots or electro magnetic anomalies had been detected by us or the equipment.

Gabreael then asked us to take a look at a couple of the pictures we earlier captured upstairs. The first was the mist in the picture we viewed earlier. The second was the same mist, but in this picture it floated across the room and stood at the foot of the bed. The mist appeared again in the last picture she had taken.

There on the screen was the perfect outline of a child. It appeared to me to be a little boy. The apparition had no features, but was a transparent silhouette of a child outlined by the mist. I could see his arms and even the outline of his little fingers.

"Camera flash, my ass!" I whispered.

~~~~~~~

"Do you know what this is?" Gabreael asked. There in her hand was what looked to me to be a small radio of some sort.

"Yes, that is an AM/FM radio." I replied.

Gabreael explained to me that, yes, it was in fact a standard pocket radio modified internally so that once placed in scan mode, it would not stop on any station as it had been originally designed
~~~~~~~

to do. She explained to me some researchers believed using the white noise, created by the continuous sweeping of the band and utilizing the internal speaker, spirits could use the radio to speak.

I thought this a very interesting device, if it could in fact be used to facilitate a real time conversation with the other side. I had my doubts, though, as I didn't see how that could actually be possible. But then again, I hadn't thought a lot of things were possible just a few short months ago.

"Have you ever received communication on it?" Athena asked.

"Yes," Gabreael replied. "A few times it has repeated my name and sometimes I hear yes or no responses to my questions."

Turning the radio on, she hit the scan button and the radio emitted a hissing sound as it swept through the am band. "Is there someone here that wishes to communicate with us?" Gabreael asked.

Our ears strained to hear the slightest reply.

"Sometimes it takes a few minutes to get a response," she enlightened us. "Is there anyone here who wishes to communicate?" she asked of no one.

Suddenly I heard a distinct female voice say, "Yes".

Was this just a fluke? Maybe some random fragment of radio broadcast somehow bled through with a seemingly direct reply to her question?

"Do you have a message for us?" Gabreael inquired.

"Yes," came the almost immediate response and it sounded like the same female voice that spoke only seconds earlier.

"What is your message?"

I was on the edge of my seat now, wanting to hear what message the voice might have for us, if any.

"Steve!" the voice shouted over the radio.

"What the hell?" I exclaimed as my coffee sloshed onto my lap.

"Did that radio just shout my name?"

"Could you repeat that for us?" Gabreael asked.

"Steve!" the female voice shouted once again.

I couldn't believe my ears.

"Can you say Athena?" Gabreael then asked, explaining she asked the spirit to repeat the name for validation we were in fact speaking with some form of intelligence.

"No… Steve," the same female voice answered.

"Well, Steve," Athena said. "Sounds like she wants to talk to you."

"Is Beverly here?" I asked.

"No, I'm Carol," was the immediate reply.

I grabbed my voice recorder from my briefcase and set it down upon the table, wanting to record any possible communication for later review. *Carol?* The voice sounded vaguely familiar.

"How many spirits are in this house?"

"Four," came the reply in the same female voice.

"How many?" I repeated the question.

"Four," was the immediate reply.

"Are there any children present here?" I asked, wondering if she could tell us the name of the little ghost boy in Gabreael's picture.

"Dumb kids… They fall down," had been the reply.

"Why is he here, Carol?" I questioned.

The next voice was not Carol's. It was a deep, male voice and sounded to be an older man. "The devil has spoken to Clay before," he clearly stated.

"Did he just say devil? Did I hear that right?" Athena asked in a shocked whisper.

"Why are you here?" I repeated the question.

"The boy brought us in here," came the reply.

Could the phantom on the radio be referring to the little ghost boy in Gabreael's photo?

"What is the child's name?" I asked, hoping to learn more from who, *or whatever,* this was we were communicating with.

"Clayton," had been the only reply.

I asked several other questions regarding the boy, but they were left unanswered. Apparently the conversation was over. The hissing of the radio was the only sound.

It was now almost four in the morning. Gabreael and Athena decided to start the next phase of the investigation.

~~~~~~~

Amelia stated earlier no one could sleep in the four poster bed upstairs. As soon as Amy would fall asleep, the bed would start to vibrate and sometimes would even shake. She said Amy would not even go upstairs by herself, she was so terrified of whatever she was convinced was up there.

"I wish she hadn't seen the pictures," Gabreael confided.

I was sure the mist Gabreael photographed earlier only served to further frighten the young girl. I had seen it in her expression, in the widening of her fearful brown eyes.

Athena volunteered to accompany Gabreael in this experiment. We went upstairs and positioned a night vision camera so it would film the large bed and hopefully capture anything that might happen to Gabreael as she slept. We then repeated the process with another camera and tri-pod in the bedroom at the end of the hallway where the little ghost boy had been photographed.

Gabreael then handed me a walkie-talkie and told me if I needed them for anything to use it to call her. I assumed Athena would be spending the night in the end bedroom, but she apparently had other plans.

"Oh, no," Athena informed me. "I'm not sleeping in here by
~~~~~~~

myself. I'm bunking with Gabreael… This is your room."

"Gee, thanks!" I sarcastically replied. My mind was weary, but the rest of me was still jacked up on caffeine. I went downstairs and retrieved Gabreael's laptop from the table in the den then went back upstairs to my room. As I walked past the camera, I hit record and then climbed into bed trying my best to get out of my clothes without making a peep show of it. I opened the laptop and turned it on. I wanted to review the pictures again and, besides, I wasn't sleepy. As I went through the folder containing the photos I noticed something in one of the shots I took.

The photo had been snapped in Amy's room. The closet door had been open and what I saw standing against the door made my jaw drop in disbelief. It was an old woman, her transparent form barely visible against the white background. Her right hand clutched her chest and she wore a wide brimmed hat. She was only visible from the waist up as the bed blocked her lower extremities. The woman had a rather distressed look on her face and I got the impression we caught her off guard as we came storming into the room with our cameras blazing. I could see every wrinkle on her weathered face.

As I carefully reviewed the remainder of the photos I spotted another anomaly we captured in Amy's bedroom. As I used the photo software on the laptop to zoom in, what I saw made me glad I wasn't sleeping in there. I noticed something in the window. It appeared in the last photo I had taken in the girl's bedroom. It was a life size face visible in the reflection of the glass. I really had to zoom in tight to make out the facial features as I had been standing approximately twenty feet away at the time the photo was taken.

There in the picture staring back at me was a face that could not have been the manifestation of anything human. And it certainly didn't appear to be transparent either. A ghastly, pale white face that had deep sunken black eyes and thin red lips drawn back in an evil grin. I could also distinctly make out what looked to be two small protrusions on the top of its head. Could those be… *Horns?*

If I wasn't sleepy before, then I damn sure wasn't now after discovering that face in the window. Should I call Gabreael and Athena and tell them about the old lady and the demonic reflection. I glanced at the walkie-talkie lying there on the night stand and decided against waking them. I already suspected Amelia had been lying to us about the Ouija board. "What in the hell has she brought into this house?" I asked of no one as I tried to find a rational explanation for what I was seeing in the picture. I slowly glanced around the dark bedroom.

Did I just see something move over there in the corner? I looked back down at the laptop and then quickly back to the corner trying to catch it off guard with a double take. I didn't see whatever it was that had darted from the corner of my eye. I thought back on the phantom voices I heard speaking through the ghost radio earlier. The way it called out my name and the familiarity of the voice identified as Carol. Could this be the same young lady haunting Lynn and I? And if so, what was she doing here now, over two hours away from home?

She said there were four spirits here. Did that number include Carol or were there four other spirits present besides her? And who was the old woman in the photo? *Just more damn questions*, I thought. I turned off the laptop and lay awake in bed just watching…listening. The beating of my heart was the only sound.

CHAPTER SEVENTEEN

"Bedeep…Bedeep… Steve, wake up!"

What the hell?

"Bedeep… Steve, are you awake?" I suddenly realized where I was and that the mysterious voice I just heard was Gabreael calling me on the walkie.

I must have ended up dozing off just a few minutes before she so rudely awoke me. I felt for the radio on the nightstand and answered her in a voice that sounded very weary to me.

She informed me it was after eight a.m. and we were to meet downstairs in the dining room at eight-thirty for breakfast. Then we would be leaving shortly after as she had a six hour drive to get back home.

Amelia turned out to be a most accommodating hostess indeed. As I headed downstairs I was greeted by the smell of bacon frying and fresh coffee being brewed.

"Are you hungry?" Amelia called.

”Yes,” I replied as I wandered into the kitchen. “I’m starved.” I made my way downstairs a few minutes early I explained, hoping to grab a cup of coffee and step outside for a smoke before breakfast.

“What do you think is here, Steve?” She suddenly inquired of me in a voice that sounded rather desperate.

“I’m not sure,” I replied as I noticed the jagged scars on her wrist as she poured my coffee. “I would feel more comfortable if you would ask Gabreael,” I explained to her. After all, this was Gabreael’s case not mine. I thanked her for the coffee and as I turned to head outside for my much needed smoke, she said something that caused me to stop in my tracks.

“I just know this is something from my past that has come back to punish me,” she said in a hushed tone as if she feared someone was listening.

“Punish you?” I questioned her. “Why would something want to punish you?” I asked as I studied the expression on her face. She didn’t wish to tell me is what it said. “I would feel more comfortable if you would talk to Gabreael about this,” I repeated.

“Yes,” she whispered. “I think I would too.”

~~~~~~~

I drove the two hours home on auto pilot, my weary mind deep in thought about everything I experienced on my first real investigation. *The little boy brought us in here* was what the ghost radio said. What exactly could that mean? Was it the same little boy I filmed in my den? Was Clayton his name? Or could it be another lost child haunting Amelia and Amy? And the familiar voice of Carol who seemed to be relaying the information over the phantom airwaves. Could that be the same Carol haunting my house? Had she and Clayton followed me to Asheville?

And for that matter, were they in the truck with me now? I
~~~~~~~

quickly glanced in the rear view mirror half-expecting to see them sitting in the backseat, but was relieved to find no one was there. *The devil has spoken to Clay before* the older man said. Could that have referred to the shadow man I attempted to banish from my home? And who was the old woman I photographed in Amy's bedroom?

All these questions swirled through my mind. Each one only seemed to raise another. And what did Amelia wish to confess to Gabreael? Whatever it was I was sure she didn't feel comfortable discussing it with me. Gabreael walked me out to my truck after breakfast. I took a few minutes to tell her about what I discovered in my pictures. I also informed her of Amelia's odd comment regarding something from her past coming back to punish her.

Gabreael thanked me for making the trip to help her and then said she planned to remain and talk with Amelia to see if she could get to the bottom of the activity. "Here, I have something for you" she said as I turned to climb into my truck. She reached into her jacket pocket and pulled out the little ghost radio. "Take this with you… You are meant to have it," she said.

"What do you mean by *meant*? I asked. And so I listened patiently as she told me everything.

How she spotted the little radio at a yard sale a few weeks ago. How she bought it on a whim and decided to attempt to modify it herself without any electrical diagram or instructions. "I just prayed that God, or whoever might be watching, would help me snip the correct wire," she stated. Then she told me about how a spirit came to her in a dream and said the radio was meant for me. "Doesn't all of this sound crazy to you?" she asked.

"Yes, it does," I confided.

But she knew I believed her. After all, knowing was her specialty.

Cruzer met me at the door and gave me that special little smile he gives when he is especially happy to see someone. “Honey, I‘m home,” I announced, suddenly reminded of Ricky Ricardo in those old *I Love Lucy* television episodes of my youth.

“How did it go?” Lynn inquired.

I told her a little about what took place on the investigation and asked her to check out the pictures still on my camera card. I loaded the card into my desktop PC and pulled up the photo of the old woman.

“What do you see?” I asked her.

“A bed, a door and… Oh, God. Is that an old woman standing in front of that closet door?” She stared at the screen in disbelief as I asked her if she wanted to see another. “Sure, why not?” she replied.

I loaded up the picture of the demonic looking reflection in the window. “What do you see?” I again asked her.

“Nothing much,” she said. “Just a vanity and a window and… What in God’s name is that?” Suddenly, she saw it. “What is that, Stephen?”

I zoomed in on the ghastly face. “You tell me,” was my only reply. I then demonstrated the ghost radio Gabreael presented to me just two hours before. “Watch this!” I told her. *I bet she’s gonna think I have finally lost it.* I pushed the power button and pressed scan.

“What is that supposed to do?” Lynn asked with a look of doubt on her face as the radio emitted its static hissing.

“It’s a ghost radio Gabreael gave me,” I told her. So she sat patiently as I explained to her what I knew about this new technology that apparently enabled the living to speak with the dead in real time. I also told her I was meant to receive it. “Hello” I said to no one in particular.

"Howdy," the female voice took a few seconds to reply.

"What is your name?" I inquired.

"Carol," came the almost immediate response.

"Carol, do you know who this is?" I asked as I pointed my finger at Lynn."

"Yes," came the reply in the same female voice.

"Rebecca Lynn," was her answer. I looked at Lynn's face to see the look of doubt replaced by one of disbelief. No one calls her by Rebecca. She has always gone by Lynn.

"Well I'm going to bed, I'm exhausted," I said to anyone listening. "Tell me bye," I giggled.

"Bye–bye," came the reply.

"So does this mean you are a… Medium?" Lynn inquired with a hint of disbelief still present in her voice.

"I don't know," I admitted. "Gabreael seems to think so… But I just don't know."

~~~~~~~

I must have slept for the better part of two days. *What day is it anyway?* I wondered through my daze. It was Monday, I decided. "Lynn?" I called. No answer. Yes, it must indeed be Monday and she already left for work. *What time is it?* I wondered as I felt for my glasses. They were not there on the nightstand where I left them. The little boy had been up to his mischief again it seemed.

I slowly climbed out of bed and limped my way into the bathroom. My back was stiff and I really didn't feel like crawling around under the bed searching for them. "I bet you think this is funny, don't you?" I said to anyone who may be listening. Just as I got seated, the phone started to ring.

"Damn it!" I swore. I rose from my porcelain perch and limped down the hallway trying to find the cordless telephone. Cruzer was curled up in his favorite recliner in the den and let out a grunt as I
~~~~~~~

limped past with my boxer shorts around my knees. “Are you laughing at me, mutt?” I was sure he was. I made my way into the kitchen and retrieved the phone from its charging cradle. Naturally, it stopped ringing just as I reached for it. I checked the caller identification information, but couldn’t see well enough to make out the name.

“Where are my damn glasses?” I shouted to no one. No answer. I limped back to the bathroom wondering just where my glasses could be hidden. “I bet you think this is hilarious,” I said as I again seated myself. As I sat there toiling I could just imagine the little ghost boy hiding somewhere watching the half-blind, half–crippled, old man with the same grin on his face he displayed in the photo from my den.

My thoughts were again interrupted by the ringing of the phone, which I now had with me in the bathroom. “Hello” I answered. It was Gabreael.

She informed me that Amelia’s confession added a new twist to the case. Apparently she had been involved in a satanic cult with her now ex-husband, who she told Gabreael was a Warlock. Gabreael went on to tell me she decided to call Sister in on the case. She emailed Sister the demonic looking reflection appearing in the window of Amy’s bedroom.

Sister referred to the thing in the photo as an *Imp*. She was convinced Amelia and Amy were dealing with pure evil and after all… Evil was her specialty.

Gabreael went on to explain how she and Athena attempted to cross over any human entities present in the house. But because of what Amelia confided to her and the demon in my photograph, she thought Sister may be required to be rid of whatever remained. Sister was already planning a trip to Asheville to confront this thing in person.

"She said you are welcome to come and join her when she arrives," Gabreael informed me.

"No, thanks," I replied as I rubbed my throbbing shoulder. "I believe I will pass on that invitation."

~~~~~~~

Originating from Germanic folklore, the imp was a small lesser demon. They were believed to be the servants of witches and warlocks where the little demons served as spies and informants, the Wikipedia article read. Could this be describing what had shown itself in my photograph? A smaller or lesser demon that shook beds and stomped its foot on the floor? Was it sent to spy on Amelia and Amy by the ex-husband? Could it have been conjured up in one of the satanic rituals they conducted? The attendants of the devil are sometimes described as imps. They are usually described as lively and having small stature, the article went on to say.

Small stature may explain why the face appeared in the bottom pane of the window. That would have made it approximately three feet in height. Whatever this thing, I was sure I didn't need to be messing around with it. I agreed with Gabreael that anything demonic would be better left to Sister. Demons were her specialty, I reminded myself as I adjusted the icepack on my aching shoulder.

I eventually located my eyeglasses that morning. Neatly folded, they had been placed on a shelf beside the dresser mirror. I would put them in the nightstand drawer from now on. Maybe that would keep them from disappearing again.

Gabreael stated I was meant to receive the ghost radio for a reason. Now, I just had to figure out what that reason might be. Did the device have something to do with my research? The diligent and systematic study of my own haunting? Only one way to find out, I concluded. My thoughts were then interrupted by a cold, wet
~~~~~~~

nose on my elbow. "Damn it, Cruzer!"

~~~~~~~

"How many spirits are here?" I asked as the radio emitted its static hiss. Maybe this technology could be used to find more answers. Or would it only result in more questions?

"There are many spirits here," came the reply. And by her voice I knew I was talking to Carol.

"Give me some names," I demanded. The reply I received made me glad I was recording it.

"Chip, Frank, Beth, Henry Hill, Courtney, Clayton, Debbie!"

And those were just the names I could hear in real time. I would discover many others later when I reviewed the recording.

"Help us!" Pleaded a male voice and it sounded desperate and distraught.

"And how can I do that?" I inquired.

"Cross us," came Carol's voice in reply.

"What did you say?" I asked her to repeat the words.

"Cross us," came the reply in a deep male voice. This was beginning to creep me out, to say the least. How many spirits were here and just what could I do to help them cross?

This radio seemed to be a party line to the other side. We had one of those when I was a boy—the one-line telephone systems of my youth. There must have been ten families on that one line. There was no such thing as a private conversation.

Anyone who wanted to could listen in. It seemed to be a pass-time for some folks. They would just pick up the receiver and quietly listen to the conversations of others who shared the party line. I could often hear them breathing. A thought suddenly occurred to me.

"Is there a portal here?" I then asked.

"A portal?" The deep male voice immediately repeated.
~~~~~~~

Was this entity actually repeating my question? I shivered as I realized that, yes, it apparently was. Then the voice that sounded like Carol's answered.

"Yes… Understand you!" Could there actually be a portal or vortex here in my home? A doorway for spirit's to use to cross from their realm into ours?

"Can you see the light?" I asked her.

"What light?" came the reply from a different male voice.

"What light?" I repeated his question. "Can you see the light?" I repeated my own.

"Yes, I found it!" came the response from what sounded like Carol.

"Then tell me goodbye as you step into the light," I instructed her. I didn't really know what I was doing. *Human spirits are of free will,* Gabreael advised. If they wished to cross, it would be up to them. All I could do was provide encouragement.

"I'm not…sure," she replied.

"You tempt me to cross it," said a male voice I had not heard before.

"Do you want to cross to Heaven?" I asked.

"Yes, Heaven… Not death," Carol replied.

"Then step into the light," I implored her.

"There's no future here… No future," her voice said.

Pray for me, I reflected back on the request that started all this. I'm an Empath, not a priest… But maybe prayer was what they needed. I bowed my head.

"Our Father, who art in heaven." I recited the Lord's Prayer. *"Hallowed be Thy name. Thy Kingdom come, Thy will be done, on Earth as it is in Heaven."* The radio went eerily silent, except for the white noise of the hissing as it swept the FM band. *"Give us this day our daily bread and forgive us of our debts as we forgive*

our debtors. Lead us not into temptation, but deliver us from evil. For Thine is the Kingdom and the power and the glory forever. Amen."

I raised my head and listened. My ears strained to hear the slightest response. The hissing of the radio was the only sound. Then suddenly Carol's voice came across the airwaves and through the speaker.

"Thank you… Goodbye..." The word goodbye trailed off as if she had fallen down a well.

Had I just freed her spirit from the prison? Had I talked her across like some Dr. Phil of the dead? Had I released her from the *in-between*? I wasn't sure, but I hoped I had. I felt like she tried to help me through all of this and I certainly wanted to return the favor. What better repayment for her efforts than the gift of everlasting life?

Power was the word Carol mentioned several times in my kitchen during our morning EVP sessions over coffee. She stated they needed *power* and said the way to help them was the light. I reflected back on the Lord's Prayer. *For Thine is the Kingdom and the power...* Could this be the power they so desperately sought?

She also mentioned that they needed my *power*. Just where I fit into this puzzle was still a mystery to me. And what about the light? These were questions I needed to find the answers to. I felt another experiment would be required to find the answers if I was to truly discover my higher purpose. Should I dare go back to the cemetery? Should I risk being followed home again by something unholy?

I was sure Sister would not have approved. *Let that aching shoulder be a reminder*, she advised. But I couldn't find the answers from here at home. And who was Henry Hill? I found this name to be most intriguing. Hill was my last name and I wondered if we could be related. *Just more damn questions!*

~~~~~~~

Yes, I knew I must go back. I'd known it from the beginning. But this time I wouldn't be asking any questions. I would just take my voice recorder and meander around the graveyard. I would not attempt to talk with them. I would just wonder around and take a few pictures. Maybe I could locate Randy Turner's grave or perhaps Henry Hill's. That would be excellent accreditation for my research. Yes, most excellent, indeed. And if anyone bothered to ask what I was doing, I would just say genealogy. I wouldn't be lying either because in a way, that's exactly what I was planning to do.

Maybe I wouldn't capture any phantom voices on my recorder. I almost hoped this would indeed be the case. Maybe all of the lingering earthbound spirits followed me home on my last visit there. Maybe I crossed them all. If some chose to remain it was beyond my control, because after all, *human spirits are of free will.* I felt the prayer helped those that did cross, though. Maybe the words *power* and *prayer* had a direct connection. Perhaps prayer was power for those who sought it.

After all, a request for prayer had been the words that started all of this. 'For this purpose was the gospel preached also to them that were dead,' I reflected back on the book of Peter. I then bowed my head and said a silent prayer of my own.

Heavenly Father, if I am still on the path, if it is Your will that I follow, please give me a sign. Please show me the way. Amen.
~~~~~~~

CHAPTER EIGHTEEN

It was a dreary morning and I wondered if I should have just stayed in bed. The wipers intermittently swept the drizzle from my windshield as I made the short drive to the cemetery. I parked on the graveyard side of the church, the lot empty except for the church bus. The office entrance was on the other side of the sanctuary so all of the staff would be parking over there. I made my way to the iron gate, only to find it locked. Old Mr. Bowers hadn't ventured out in the drizzle to unlock it, I figured. After all, who would be calling on the interred on such a dreary, weekday morning? My back groaned in protest as I stepped over the stone wall.

The place held a surreal feeling as I slowly wandered through the wet rows of stone, my recorder in hand. I searched for the tombstones of the spirits that gave me first and last names. I had my camera handy in case I actually found one of them. They would be a valuable validation for my research and validation was something

I felt was needed. So far I was having no luck, but at least the drizzle subsided.

Many of the headstones had fallen over, the inscriptions worn away by the seasons. Even things etched in stone cannot forever endure the passing of the ages. Like the innocence of a child, they are worn away a little at a time–day by day, week by week, month by month… Year by year. I continued my search, deep in thought, as I scanned the stones still readable for familiar names. The sky began to lighten and the sun peeked through a little opening in the clouds. White mist soon began to rise from the wet grass and headstones as the sunlight warmed my face. It appeared as if all the spirits there were rising up from the graves.

A sudden feeling of enlightenment swept over me as I watched the misty tendrils floating up from the stones. Could this be the sign I asked for? I stood there mesmerized by the mist as it ascended towards the heavens. Just about then I thought I heard laughter. It was the faint but unmistakable giggle of a child.

I quickly turned and glanced around, half-expecting to find someone standing close by. No one was there… I was completely alone. A chill ran down my already aching spine and the now familiar sensation of crawling skin slowly began to creep over me. I reflected back on the disembodied voice that caused the hasty retreat on my last visit there and decided it was time for me to leave.

I made my way back toward the cemetery gate. I tried to make myself believe the laughter had been just a figment of my imagination, glancing back over my shoulder as I went. As I was stepping back over the cemetery wall, I could have sworn I heard the faint laughter once more. I quickly turned again to find no one was there.

"Do not follow me!" I insisted to no one. "Stay here in the

graveyard." As I was about to pull out of the driveway I looked down at the ghost radio lying there on the passenger seat. I hadn't planned on verbally communicating on this visit but I just couldn't resist the urge to turn it on. I stopped the truck and hit the scan button. The radio emitted its now familiar hiss as it swept the band waves.

"Is anybody here in the truck with me?" I casually asked. My ears strained to hear the slightest response.

"Of course we are here," was the only reply.

I was sure they, whoever they were, followed me home. I called Gabreael and informed her of my experiences that morning and of the laughter of the child which sounded to me to be a very young girl. I indeed recorded a giggling, little, ghost girl on my recorder.

"That is not an EVP" Gabreael advised. "If you can hear it through your mortal ears as it is spoken, it is considered a disembodied voice, or sound, not electronic voice phenomena," she enlightened me. "Did you hear anything else audibly?" She asked.

"No, but listen to this," I excitedly told her. I put the phone up to the computer speaker and hit play on the editing software. The voices of many children came through the speaker loud and clear. It sounded as if I had been surrounded by them. Could they have been the cause of the creepy sensations that prematurely ended my search for the headstones? I was in the far corner of the graveyard when the voices were recorded. It sounded as if I wandered into some kind of daycare of the dead. The children said many things to me and I sat listening in disbelief, sure Gabreael was doing the same.

"Momma," cried the first little voice and sounded like one of those talking baby dolls my sister played with as a child.

The next was the voice of a toddler, a very young boy. "I want Daddy," had been his message.

I wondered if these innocent voices were having the same emotional effect on Gabreael as they were on me.

"I'm crying," came the next voice, and it indeed sounded as if the young girl was crying.

Then came a most disturbing request from an older sounding child. She sounded to be around ten or so. "Watch us scream," were the words she clearly spoke.

Then the shrill voice of a very young girl. "Much power... Take us home," which was followed by the little giggle I audibly heard.

Much *power?* Could this have been in reference to me? Next on the recorder, another young boy spoke. What he said brought tears to my eyes.

"It's Father, I'll go home." This was followed by what sounded to be a chorus of many small voices repeating the phrase, *go home*.

I was suddenly reminded of the words of Christ as written in the verse of Mark 10:14. "Let all the little children come unto me, and do not hinder them, for the kingdom of God belongs to such as these."

The last little voice asked a question that caused the tears to spill freely down my face. "Mister... Don't you like us?" The boy cried with a tone of great disappointment in his pitiful voice as I was hastily walking away.

"What have I stumbled into Gabreael?" I asked her, trying to hide the fact I was now sobbing. The precious voices of innocence affected me as an Empath and also as a parent. "Why did they all come to me?" I questioned through my tears.

"You are of pure heart. They could see your light and were drawn to it like moths to a candle," she enlightened me. "You are extremely gifted, Stephen. Your abilities are of the highest degree."

I still had trouble digesting all this and hoped my house hadn't become a romper room for these ghost kids. *Well, at least Clayton would have some playmates, if he was in fact still here with me.* Or maybe he crossed into the light with Carol. I hoped he had. Yes, if the Kingdom of God does belong to such as these, I truly hoped he had.

"Why have all these children not crossed over Gabreael?" I asked, still wiping at the tears leaving their salty trails down my cheeks and onto my bottom lip. "Why do they linger in the graveyard? And what should I do to try to help them?" I implored her to tell me as my mind whirled with questions.

"I think you know the answers," was her thoughtful reply. "They are lost and afraid. They were telling you, did you not hear them?"

She answered my questions with one of her own. "I'm crying… Watch us scream. Much power, take us home. It's Father, I'll go home," she repeated the words of the children. "They were telling you, Steve. Listen… You already have the answers!"

~~~~~~~

Yes, it seemed my latest field trip indeed resulted in answers. Now I just needed to figure out exactly what the questions might be. Were these little souls just lost? Could they not find the way to the light? Or were they trapped there with their headstones in some realm *in-between?* Were they held against their will by *something unseen?* Controlled by some dark force that didn't wish to let them go?

On the recorder, I heard another voice I missed before. It was a deep male voice and, although it was very faint, I could clearly hear what it said through my headphones. It spoke just after the little boy said, *It's Father, I'll go home.* What it said raised new questions.

"No children… You cannot go home!" The voice sounded as if it were scolding them. Could this be a parent figure that watched
~~~~~~~

over these children of the grave? Or could it be a dark force that held them there in that quiet place of the dead? *Fear the demons,* flashed through my mind as I pondered this new theory.

The children seemed very glad to see me; yes, very glad indeed. Was I the one who could free them? Was it I who held the keys to the eternal prison? Maybe they hadn't followed me home after all. Maybe they were still waiting there, crying, screaming, hoping I would return and free them from whatever entity prevented them from entering the light of Heaven. I would have to go back… The children demanded it!

I glanced down at the small, gray radio lying on my desk. I hesitantly picked it up and hit the power button. The radio emitted its static hiss as it swept the FM band.

"Who's here with me now?" I asked, half-hoping I wouldn't receive a reply, although I already knew I would.

"Courtney," the young lady answered.

"Courtney, why are you here?" I casually inquired.

"They ask for children," sounded the voice from another female I never heard before.

"What children?" I prodded. Then she responded with a plea that again caused my tears to flow.

"We lost them," she said. "We must get them back… Help us!" She pleaded in a voice so desperate, so overcome with grief I could feel the sadness emanating from the speaker.

"And what can I do to help them?" I wondered out loud. I wanted to help this young woman who apparently lost her children, but I still wasn't sure what I should do. "Where are the children?" I inquired.

"In the stones," came her reply.

I guessed she was referring to the cemetery. "Why are they there?" I wanted to know.

"They are trapped," came the answer from Courtney.

"Are you in this house with me?" I questioned the voice.

"Yes," the immediate reply.

"How many are here?" I prodded.

"There are many here," she informed me.

"Why do they come?" I continued with my questions. They were in a talkative mood and I wanted all the answers they were willing to give.

"I need your empathic," cried a deep male voice.

"So you can see what I am?" I questioned.

"Yes," was the immediate reply from the same voice.

"Spirit Empath who…helps us," were the words he so clearly spoke.

Gabreael referred to me as an *Empath*. I reflected back on the EVP I recorded on one of my earlier field trips which now seemed eons ago. The voice in the cemetery referred to me as the *Spirit Man*. Now, according to the voice on the ghost radio I was a *Spirit Empath.*

"So I am a Spirit Empath?" I prodded, still trying to understand exactly what he was telling me.

"You are *THE Empath!*" the deep, male voice exclaimed. "You must help us… We're not dead!"

Yes, my new theory now seemed to take on a life of its on. According to the ghosts on my radio, many were seeking my help. The requests seemed to vary from voice to voice. Some wanted prayer, some asked for children and others just wanted to convey a message. Some asked for help to cross, while others just asked for coffee. I guess the vices we crave in our mortal lives must carry over with us into the hereafter. One male voice had even stated he took his coffee with cream and asked for a 'Winston'. *This was rather an odd request*, I thought. Yes, rather odd….indeed.

"I drink mine black," I informed him.

"Yuck," the immediate reply.

"How about a Marlboro?" I offered as I fired one up and took a deep drag.

"Smell's like crap," had been his response just after I exhaled a billowing cloud of smoke.

Oh great, a ghost with a sense of humor. The dead comedians, I thought as I reflected back on Maps and Joe. "Hey Joe, is that an EMF meter in your pocket, or are you just glad to see me?" I could imagine them asking him. I found the notion hilarious.

"So you miss creamed coffee and Winstons?" I half-asked and half-chuckled the question.

"Yes," confided the same voice.

"And chocolate," added a female.

Like I mentioned before, this radio seemed to be a party line to the other side. Many voices tried to speak at once and I was having trouble keeping up because they were now speaking over each other. This was beginning to overwhelm my auditory senses.

"Be quiet!" I suddenly shouted. "Wait your turn," I commanded.

"Yeah, I can talk," snapped a female and I could detect a note of sarcasm in her voice.

Then spoke the voice of what sounded to me like a young girl. She sounded to be around twelve of so. "Let me talk," she requested, of exactly whom I wasn't sure. "Oh… I hear myself!" She exclaimed with a tone of pure amazement in her voice.

"What is your name, young lady?" I casually inquired. "Can you tell me how old you are?"

"Megan Aretha…" came the almost immediate reply. I'm old… twelve," she giggled.

Now it was I who was amazed as I suddenly realized this young spirit was truly surprised to hear her own voice emitting through the speaker of the radio. She was apparently as intrigued by this new form of communication as I was. She seemed very eager to say more so I figured I would just keep on asking questions while I had her.

"Do you know my dog's name?" I questioned.

"Cruzer," an older female stated so clearly it sent goose bumps running down my arms. "Could you say that again?" I asked, still not believing my ears. I was glad I thought to record all of this! Gabreael would want to hear it, I was sure.

"Wait… Is it...Cruzer?" The dead comedian inquired .with an unmistakable tone of amusement in his voice. "He's a mutt," he then added.

Smart ass, I thought to myself. "Do you play with Cruzer?" I prodded.

"Uh-ha… Try to push him…and pull him," giggled another little ghost girl. "Dogs must play," she thoughtfully added in the sweetest little voice.

"Stop, Debbie," instructed an older sounding female. Could the little ghost girl be named Debbie? So maybe that's why Cruzer spent so much time curled up under my desk, I reasoned. He was trying to get away from the little girl who pushed him. "Are there dog's in your realm?" I asked, hoping the answer would be yes.

"I have a crazy cat," the little girl replied.

"Meoooooow!" screeched the ghost box. "Your cat is dead… can't run…meooooow! The dead comedian voice screeched again. Then I heard the voice snicker as it mewed again.

"Why don't you just turn this stuff off?" inquired a much older sounding female voice.

"Useless they talk," came the comedic voice again.

I didn't think it was useless, though. I was collecting valuable data for my research. The diligent and systematic study of my newly discovered ability to communicate with the other side.

"Does a mad man realize he is insane?" I asked the question I still had no answer for.

"Time will tell," was the comedic reply.

The session left me somewhat shaken to say the least. There seemed to be so many different voices. All with their own thoughts and opinions, they were not hesitant to relay through the radio. I sat in my chair several minutes trying to absorb all I heard.

Were all these ghosts already here in my house, or could they come and go at will through the portal? Was this portal they spoke of here all the time? Or did it open and close, somehow trapping them in this realm… My living room? Just more damn questions to ponder. But at least now I had a direct line of communication to try to find the answers.

They said they played with Cruzer, which is what he had been trying to tell me in his own way. I looked down at my feet to find him in his usual hiding place under my desk. "It's okay, boy," I softly told him. I will tell them to leave you alone."

The look he gave me seemed to hint he didn't quite believe they would. If a dog can roll his eyes, then he did in that look.

I loaded my recording into the computer and donned my headphones. I was certain the noise of the radio bothered him, it even started to give me a headache. All the hiss and static can be annoying until you get used to it. As the audio played on I could hear many things I missed in real time.

Some of the replies were much louder than others. Those seemed to be the ones I heard and responded to. But there were fainter voices, down under the hiss. They were clear, as well, but much harder to hear as they spoke—so many were talking at once. I was just learning, I realized. I was just touching the tip of the iceberg. Just viewing a small glimpse of something larger. *Something yet unseen.* Maybe a higher understanding, or maybe pure insanity. Sometimes I'm not sure which, but time will surely tell.

~~~~~~~

Gabreael called that evening after I sent her the recording from the session via email. She told me the clip was outstanding for the information it contained. "You are an electronic communicator," she informed me.

"Meaning exactly what?" I asked her.

"You don't hear them like I do, for example," she said. You hear them through the use of electronic devices such as the ghost radio. You give them a voice for everyone to hear. Steve, you are what is known as an Electronic Medium, and a very gifted one," she enlightened me.

So, now I was a medium of sorts. I couldn't really argue the fact. I asked questions and received direct responses on several occasions. I couldn't help but snicker at the sound of this terminology. "Electronic Medium," I repeated the words out loud. "What am I, some—DJ of the dead?" I chuckled.

"Yes," she answered. "In a way you are." She went on to inform me that Sister thwarted the demon plaguing Amelia and Amy up in Asheville. Sister said the evil presence was gone. And after all, evil is her specialty!

I hope she indeed had, for their sake. I wasn't so sure about the human spirits, though. After all, they are of free will and cannot be ousted through religious provocation, such as a demon-stalking Nun. Or maybe they had all followed me home. It seemed to be the *in* thing to do with them lately.

Gabreael then asked me if I wanted to try an experiment.

"Sure," I replied.
~~~~~~~

Her idea was to take me to an overnight investigation in Moundsville, West Virginia. "It is rumored to be haunted by the spirits of the former inmates," she informed me. "The West Virginia State Prison," she added.

~~~~~~~

Spirits in prison, the words from the book of Peter sounded in my head. I researched the name online and found the prison was built in 1866, the year after the Civil War ended. It was famous for being one of the most violent prisons in our country's history. I also read an article that stated the inmates believed if they should die inside those walls their spirits would be forever imprisoned there. Doomed to serve an eternal sentence from which there is no chance of parole.

The article stated this belief was so strong the warden would send terminally ill inmates to the town hospital during their final days, so they wouldn't have to die inside the prison. Apparently the guards and staff shared this belief. The inmates who faced execution were not so fortunate, nor were the ones who died by the hands of fellow inmates. Many reports of ghostly apparitions and phantom sounds or voices have been documented there.

"I want to take you there, all expenses paid," Gabreael said. "I want to see what you can get on your recorder." She also said she signed me up to conduct a ghost radio session as a demonstration for other investigators who would be in attendance.

"So we would be spending the night in the prison?" I inquired.

"Yes! We'll be locked in the place all night," she informed me.

I found the idea very exciting and accepted her invitation with gratitude. It would be a great opportunity to get out of the house and a chance to further my research in a very historic location. I had no way of knowing then, but this would be one trip I would never forget.
~~~~~~~

CHAPTER NINETEEN

"Is there someone here who can communicate on this device?" Our ears strained to hear the slightest response.

The static hissing of the radio was interrupted by a loud, "Yes".

"What is your name," I casually asked of no one.

"Careful," the same male voice warned.

"Careful?" I questioned.

No reply.

"What is your name?"

A few seconds went by before the reply was spoken. I could see a short, bald guy sitting on the front row of the large room deep inside the prison. He rolled his eyes and I could see the expression on his face—an expression of skepticism. 'I don't believe in this shit!' that look said.

"I'm Vick... That's Roy," the voice suddenly answered.

"Did anyone hear that?" I asked of the small group.

"I did," acknowledged a young man I could barely see in the

dim light.

"What is your name, sir?" I then asked the bald guy on the front row.

"Who me?" he replied with a look of amusement on his face. "I'm Fred," he stated.

"Say hi to Fred," I asked of no one.

"Hi, Fred," was the almost immediate response. It sounded to be the same male voice. The one calling himself Vick.

The man's eyes widened at the sound of his name being spoken.

"They say hi, Fred," I repeated for his verification. He slowly started to shake his head as if having trouble believing his own ears. "Fred doesn't believe in this form of communication," I chuckled. "I don't think he heard you."

"FRED!" The voice then shouted through the speaker.

I watched the man's shoulders slump and could see the color leaving his face. I think he was in shock.

"Why are you here?" I questioned. Everyone sat on the edge of their seats listening for any possible response.

"It's prison here," came Vick's voice through the static.

"Why are you here?" Gabreael repeated my question.

"It's prison here, free us!" came the reply.

"I heard that too!" exclaimed the young man.

"What is your name, son?" I asked him.

"Ryan," he stated.

"Can you say hi to Ryan?" I asked.

"Hi Ryan," came the immediate reply.

"Is there a message you wish to relay, Vick?" I asked.

"We are trapped here," was his answer.

"I heard that!" exclaimed an older lady seated in the back row of the small group. I could not see her in the dim light, but she sounded to be around sixty or so.

"He said they are trapped here," said another female in the group. This was the first time I conducted a session in a public setting and I was pleased the audience was hearing the responses in real time, without me prompting them. The small, electric lantern sitting on the table in front of me dimmed suddenly and then came back on. "Was that you Vick, did you just dim my lantern?" I questioned.

"I like power," said the voice from the radio.

"Why do you need power?" I asked hoping to learn why they always seemed to seek it.

Just about then I glanced up to see the scariest thing I had witnessed thus far on this investigation.

~~~~~~~

A young woman seemingly just appeared out of the darkness. She was dressed in all black and I could see she was several months pregnant. I could make out numerous tattoos on her neck and arms in the dim light of the lantern. I then noticed she wore a ring in her nose and her bottom lip was decorated with some sort of pin stuck through it. She walked in front of my table and cleared her throat as if she were going to address the group. I thought maybe she had a question.

"May I help you, miss?" I inquired.

"Stop this racket," she hissed through clenched teeth.

"Excuse me?" I replied, wondering what this little Goth girl's problem could be.

"Stop all of this noise!" She hissed again. I could feel the hostility emanating from her. "We are trying to have a séance down the hall and this noise is interrupting us!" She then informed me in a not so friendly tone.

"Oh, well excuse me, young lady. I am sorry if we're being too
~~~~~~~

loud," I told her in a calm voice. I tried my best not to return her rudeness. "We are finishing up the demonstration in just a few minutes," I assured her.

"You've already pissed off half of my group! I want you to stop this now!" She shouted, not even trying to hide the hatred in her voice.

Suddenly, I lost it. How rude could a person be? "Well why don't you bring the other half of your group in here so I can piss them off as well?" I asked her. "I was asked here to do this demonstration of real time communication using this device, and that's all I'm doing," I assured her in a not so friendly tone of my own.

"If you don't stop this noise immediately, I will have the staff here make you stop!" she screamed as she made her exit back to wherever the hell she came from.

As she walked away I said, "Good bye."

"Bitch!" added the voice on the radio.

The room erupted in laughter as they heard the response in real time.

"And with that we will conclude the demonstration," I announced. I wouldn't want my direct communication with the deceased inmates to mess up a séance, now would I?

~~~~~~~

Our equipment was set up on a table in this one room. We decided at least one of us should stay with it at all times. Gabreael brought a laptop, cameras, another ghost box and various other equipment—too much gear to carry during our investigation of various areas in the immense prison.

The groups were getting organized to begin the hunt and an air of excitement filled the place. Others gave demonstrations of equipment such as EMF meters, motion detection devices, and
~~~~~~~

some tips on EVP and photography.

I volunteered to take first watch over the equipment table. Gabreael and Athena took their recorders and cameras and set out down the long, dark corridor. The young man who introduced himself as Ryan lingered behind the others present for the demonstrations. He looked to be around eighteen or so. I asked him to have a seat at the table with me. I could tell he had something on his mind.

He explained he was a senior in high school and decided to do a paper on the history of the prison for a school project. The more he studied and learned about the place, the more fascinated he became with the intimidating castle-like structure that once housed some of the nation's most violent criminals. This led to his paying to attend a guided tour of the facility where he heard rumors of paranormal activity from one of the tour staff. He then befriended the staff member and eventually was offered a job on the night shift at the prison on weekends. He jumped at the opportunity to work in the penitentiary and especially the chance to be inside at night.

"Can I get your opinion on something?" he asked as he pulled a small digital recorder from his pocket.

"Sure," I replied.

So he told me that on Friday of the previous weekend he stayed after all the overnight visitors left. He made his usual rounds to make sure all the exterior doors were secure as part of his duties. Hoping to capture an EVP, he had his recorder around his neck on a lanyard and left it recording as he made his way through the dark cell blocks.

"What does this sound like to you?" He asked me as he hit play on the recorder.

KA-BOOM sounded through the speaker as the shotgun blast echoed through the prison.

"I know exactly what that sounds like," I informed him. "Did you hear that audibly?" I asked him.

"Yes sir," he stated. "I heard it loud and clear. I checked the whole prison after I quit screaming and calmed down," he confided. "I was locked in, not a living soul was in here, I swear!"

"That is incredible," I told him. I took the recorder and patched it into Gabreael's laptop so I could run it through her editing software. I listened to the blast several times through a set of headphones. It was very loud and I could definitely tell it was a shotgun blast from inside the building.

"That's a 12 gauge, semi-automatic, shotgun," I informed him.

"How can you tell?" He questioned me with a puzzled look on his young face.

"I can hear the empty shell hit the floor and bounce across the concrete." I enlightened him, "If it had been a pump action shotgun it would have made a specific noise as the pump was operated to eject the shell. I don't hear that, so it is a semi-auto shotgun."

We both agreed that was an amazing phantom sound he captured on his recorder. Then he asked me about my ghost radio and wanted to know more about the technology and what tips I could offer him as to its use. We exchanged email addresses. I promised I would get in touch with him the following week if I captured anything good on my audio from this visit. And I said I would help him anyway I could. Little did I know then, it would be he who would be helping me.

~~~~~~~

Our conversation was interrupted just then by the distant sounds of women screaming.

"What the hell?" I exclaimed as I listened to the horrific screams echoing down the empty cell blocks.

"Probably just found the bats," Ryan laughed. "I better go and
~~~~~~~

see if I can rescue them," he sighed.

"Who, the bats or the women?" I chuckled in reply. It seems the prison is still inhabited by some living creatures of the night… Not just the dead.

Gabreael and Athena came shuffling out of the darkness. They were moving at a much faster rate than during their departure thirty minutes earlier.

"Freaking bats!" Athena swore.

They were the cause of the ghastly screams we heard just a few minutes before. I couldn't help but chuckle as they stood before me in the dim light, wide eyed, and disheveled with their hair somewhat awry. Just then we heard another series of screams echoing from a distant area of the prison. Another group must have wandered into the section known as the bat cave. A cell block that seemed to be a preferred hangout for the winged creatures of the night.

Gabreael said they were ready to take a break from investigating and it was my turn for a while.

I grabbed my camera, recorders, and flashlight then set out down the dark corridor. I could hear other investigators talking as I entered a cell block and then saw the distant flashes from their cameras as they conducted their own investigations. Since I was after audio evidence, I knew I would need to distance myself from the others and find a quiet place to record. I also needed a smoke. There was no smoking allowed inside the prison. I followed the red exit signs until I reached an exterior door.

I stepped out into the cool, night air to find myself standing in the north yard of the prison. I hit the record button on my tape recorder and lit up a smoke. Far across the huge yard, I could see a gatehouse. The words *North Wagon Gate* were painted over the archway. I read that this building also served as the gallows for the prison, until they got an electric chair in 1923. I stood there enjoying my cigarette as I imagined just what it must have felt like to be blindfolded and led up those stairs knowing you were climbing to your death.

CHAPTER TWENTY

The gatehouse contained a second story where I, the prisoner, would be placed over a trap door in the floor. The prison chaplain would be there with me, asking God's forgiveness for the sins that condemned me to this fate, as the noose was placed around my neck. Then the waiting began—for the sound of the lever being pulled and the trap door swinging from under my feet. And knowing all along the executioner will not set me free from this hell. Condemned to serve an eternal sentence—haunting this hell-hole forever. For I am about to die inside these walls and that is the thing I fear the most… Even more than death itself. Then the snap of my neck breaking is the last sound I ever hear....

I shivered as a cool breeze passed over me and chased away my imagining. I hit the stop button on my recorder and replayed the three minutes of audio just recorded. My headphones hung around my neck. I put them on and plugged them into the unit. What I heard sent another round of shivers down my spine.

Tormented screams made up of many voices—all of them sounded male. I wondered if they were the screams of the inmates who died in this place of incarceration. They trailed off with the wind on the tape, like phantom voices often do. I decided this was a sign. They were letting me know they were there… That they could never leave. My vision seemed so real, so first person, so terrifying. Could I have been feeling the emotions and fears of the condemned? I wasn't quite sure, but I couldn't help think, yes .. I just might have.

~~~~~~~

I stopped as I neared the gatehouse gallows and decided to snap a photo. I wanted it mainly as a memento of my trip. I aimed the camera up high enough to get the trap door and stairway into the shot. I also wanted to capture most of the outside of the formidable looking building. The camera flashed as I clicked the shutter. I reviewed the photo on the small display screen of the camera.

I noticed, inside the gatehouse, a large green orb was visible in the picture. It seemed to be floating mid-way up the stairs. *Holy crap!* I thought to myself. I zoomed in on the sphere of greenish light. I raised the camera and took another shot trying to duplicate the picture just taken. The orb was gone in this frame, or if it was there, it was no longer visible.

I slowly walked through the huge arched entrance and into the death house. I placed my tape recorder on the sill of the narrow slit of a window at the bottom of the stairs. I fished my digital recorder out of my pocket and stood directly under the gallows trap door.

"Is there anyone here in this place?" I casually asked. "Does someone wish to speak with me?" I inquired.

Suddenly I heard a *thump* from out of nowhere. It reminded me of the sound a heavy boot would make on a wooden floor, like the one in the attic. *The attic?* I thought to myself as my shoulder
~~~~~~~

throbbed. *Hell no, I wasn't about to go up there.* Besides the prison staff warned us against going up there during the orientation tour they led us on upon our arrival.

The stairway was rather rickety looking and then there was the trap door in the floor. If you accidentally stepped on that in the dark it might open and drop you onto the hard concrete twenty-five feet below. No, I didn't think anyone could be up there and was hoping the recorders were picking up what I heard. Several more slight thumps or footsteps could be heard overhead.

I stayed there several more minutes, just standing under the trap door and listening for any further sounds. Suddenly, I heard the crunch of footsteps on gravel and realized other investigators were approaching the gatehouse. I decided to try my luck elsewhere.

The little pregnant Goth girl arrived with the rest of her coven in tow. One of them carried what looked to be an Ouija board under her arm. I nodded at them as I made my exit, but no one bothered to return it. They just stared at me as I walked by. *Gee, I must have pissed them all off after all.*

~~~~~~~

I made my way back inside the prison and decided to check on Gabreael and Athena. I retraced my steps through the empty cell blocks down the pitch black corridors to our equipment table. They had packed up most of the equipment and informed me they were about ready to call it a night.

"We will take one short look around the south wing and then we'll be ready to go," Gabreael said and I could hear the weariness in her voice.

It had been a long night already, nearing four in the morning. I really couldn't blame them after their encounter with the bats and all.

"Stay low," I chuckled as they were walking into the darkness.
~~~~~~~

I donned my headphones and listened to the digital audio from the gatehouse. I hoped to hear the phantom thumps or footsteps on the recording, but it didn't seem to have picked them up. Maybe my tape recorder captured them, I thought.

"Oh, shit!" I swore to no one as I suddenly realized I left my tape recorder in the window of the gatehouse. I forgot it in my haste to get away from the negative vibes and hateful stares of the Goth girl and her entourage. There had not been a happy looking person in the whole lot of them. Hateful looking, yes, happy looking… No. *Hope they don't steal the damn thing*, I thought.

I couldn't leave our equipment unattended so I would just have to wait until Gabreael and Athena returned before I could go retrieve it. I continued to listen to my digital recordings to find I captured a couple of voice anomalies while in the gatehouse and another on my way back through the deserted cell block. The first male voice spoke in response to my question, *Is there anybody here in this place? Hello,* he had replied. Then when I asked, *does anyone wish to speak with me?* he replied with, *we are having fun now.*

The voice wasn't just a whisper, but a deep, human–sounding, male voice. *Having fun?* Could he be referring to the strange colored orb in my picture and the phantom footsteps from the attic? Was this their idea of fun? Hanging around in the building they were hung in?

"Would you help us?" Spoke a clearly female voice from the recorder.

I remembered the tour guide mentioned there were women housed at the prison during the 1970's in a separate barracks-type facility no longer in existence. And as far as I can determine, no women were ever executed there. I had no idea who she might have been, or what she was doing there in the gatehouse.

The third anomalous voice spoke as I was walking back inside the prison. “Clean your blanket,” the male voice clearly said.

I wished I had more time there. I wanted to go back to the cell block where he chose to utter these words. Maybe he would have something else to say. I didn’t feel he had been talking to me, though. It sounded like something one would say to a cell mate.

My reviewing was then interrupted by Ryan who told me the prison would be closing in less than thirty minutes. He also asked me if I found anything good to tell him about my investigation.

I played the EVP from the cell block for him and watched a look of amazement overtake his serious expression. I then told him I needed to go and retrieve my recorder from the gatehouse window.

“I’ll run and get it,” he offered.

I thanked him as he disappeared into the darkness.

CHAPTER TWENTY-ONE

Cruzer had been especially glad to see me. I had been his constant companion for many months now and he probably thought I would never come back. He greeted me with his happy smile and did a little doggie dance as I walked through the front door.

Lynn said he'd been very restless while I was in Moundsville. He roamed our small house searching for me every morning when he got out of bed. Then he would sit the rest of the day staring out the window, watching for me to return.

I spotted him there when I pulled into the drive. Where had his servant gone? Why would he leave him all alone for three days? 'Doesn't he realize I need him here to wait on me? To top off my water bowl and scoop up my poop? Doesn't he know I miss him?' The little dog in the window just couldn't understand. *Yes, he must surely love me.* I thought this as he jumped up on me, almost knocking me over.

The prison investigation had been quite an experience, to say the least. I told Lynn all about the trip then decided I needed to get some sleep. I was very tired from the excursion and all I experienced inside the penitentiary. I hadn't slept a wink in almost forty eight hours.

Gabreael and Athena went back to the hotel where we were staying and slept for the better part of the day after we left the prison. I just sat alone in my room, watching television and drinking the complimentary coffee.

I tried to go to sleep, but my mind wouldn't let me rest. As soon as I would doze off I would again be standing on that trap door, with a black shroud over my head, the noose around my neck. Waiting for the hangman to pull the lever, listening to hear the sound of my neck snapping. The last sound I would ever hear through these mortal ears.

Each time I sat straight up in bed, gasping for breath, my hair damp with sweat. I talked non-stop on the way back to North Carolina. Athena couldn't get a word in edgewise. I guess it was all the coffee I drank.

But now I was tired and just wanted to check my email before I popped a sleeping pill and sailed off into a dreamless coma. I remembered the tape recorder Ryan ran and got for me from the gatehouse. I hadn't reviewed the audio from the recorder yet, but it could wait until whatever day I decided to wake up again.

I stared at the computer screen through bleary eyes, as I checked my account for mail. The only email had been from the camera store, announcing a sale on cameras and accessories. This made me think of the picture I snapped of the gatehouse and the strange looking green orb floating over the stairs. I retrieved my camera from my briefcase and plugged the memory card into my computer. I pulled up the picture of the orb and zoomed in on the sphere of pale, green light.

"Dust my ass," I said to no one. Then I pulled up the picture I had taken just after, where the orb seemed to disappear. I scanned the picture as closely as I could through my weary eyes. No trace of the orb, though.

Then I saw something I missed before. Just at the bottom of the shot was something solid. I zoomed in on this anomaly to discover I was looking into the eyes of a ghost! I aimed the camera up to get the trap door in the shot. Down at the bottom of the frame, I captured a head from the chin up. The face was outlined by long, thick, black, matted hair. Heavy black eyebrows, a mustache, and a goatee were also clearly visible.

Now I was wide awake! I rubbed my eyes and looked at the face again. It seemed to be from another time, another era. I couldn't believe what I saw staring back at me. His eyes weren't lifeless and cold, but sorrowful... Remorseful. I could almost feel the pain as I studied the expression on his face. It was the look of a tormented soul. Could this be one of the condemned inmates who had been hanged in the gatehouse?

"Lynn... Come in here," I shouted.

I pointed my finger at the ghost in my new picture. She could also see the ghastly face staring back at us on the screen. I searched through my briefcase until I found Ryan's email address. I wrote to him, asking if he would check out the gatehouse for me to see if he could find any rational explanation for what I photographed in there just a few hours ago. I also sent him the picture of the phantom head.

I just wish I had aimed the camera lower. I might have gotten more of the ghostly inmate. Maybe he was wearing prison stripes. Judging from the picture, the head was at the right height for him to have been sitting on the floor with his back propped against the corner of the room. Who he was, I may never know. I did know one thing, though. If I was ever meant to take a ghost picture, then this was certainly it!

~~~~~~~

Gabreael's experiment had indeed been a fruitful one. In a six hour period, I managed to make contact using the ghost radio, by standard EVP, and even captured a ghostly face on my camera. I emailed her the pictures and EVPs from the trip and she, in turn forwarded all of it to Sister.

Of course Sister said everything I got was demonic. Everything was a demon in her view. She didn't believe in a realm *in-between*, just angels and demons in an eternal battle for souls. I realized because of this, I would never be of the Greek Orthodox faith. Those were her beliefs, not mine.

I didn't only believe in this unseen realm, I had proof it existed. At least to me it was proof that, yes, a form of consciousness does survive the mortal body long after it has turned to dust. A form of intelligence that wishes to make itself known to us, the living.

Yes, the experiment gave further validation to my research, and validation was what I felt was still needed. Were these the voices of deceased inmates forever trapped inside the concrete walls and steel bars? Or was the Nun correct in her theory that they were all demonic entities just telling me what they thought I wanted to hear. Masquerading as children in a cemetery, or as a young couple in my den? Or maybe as an inmate in the gallows of a West Virginia prison or a mist in a photo from my childhood?

~~~~~~~

No, I wasn't Presbyterian anymore. They don't believe in a place *in-between* or demons that plague the souls of both the living and deceased. I didn't think I was meant to be Catholic either. I just felt wouldn't fit in well. Maybe one day I will find a religion that encompasses in its beliefs all I now know as fact. Until then I will be a soul *in-between*, because that is where my subject of interest dwells.

They asked me for help at the prison, though, while I was alone there in the gatehouse and also during my ghost radio demonstration. Could I have set these spirits free from their eternal confinement? I was already making plans to return there. My research demanded it! Should I attempt to cross them to the light of Heaven? Or are they there in that place by some design—some purpose I was not meant to know or understand? *Just more damn questions!*

~~~~~~~

But I could not find the answers without going back… Without asking the questions, if I could figure out what the questions really were. So, I believe in spirits of the living and demons from down under. I believe in angels that serve in heaven and the devil that reigns in hell. Of course I believe in God the Father, the Creator… the Power and the Light. And I also believe, based on my research that all of them can and do walk this earth and interject into our lives. For whether we choose to believe in demonic entities or not, Sister and those on the other side certainly do… They warn about them constantly.

The tape recorder audio from the gatehouse proved interesting to say the least. Yes, it indeed captured the phantom footsteps I heard audibly while I was there. It recorded something else as well…a séance. The coven apparently did not notice it sitting there on the window sill, bearing silent witness. I could imagine them sitting on the floor in a circle, the Ouija board at the center. Their fingers would lightly touch the oracle as they asked questions of the spirit. Ouija boards have been around for over a century and are said to enable communication with the dead. But unlike the ghost radio or EVP, the spirits spell out what they want to say using an
~~~~~~~

oracle or planchette. Assuming the ghost could spell, of course.

Sister and Gabreael both advised against its use, though. Gabreael was not so much against the communication itself, but rather the method used to receive it. The oracle cannot move without human and spirit interaction, meaning in a way you are asking the spirit to use you to spell out the message. Never a good idea. Sister also advised against it because the users are inviting the entity to possess them.

The boards are imprinted with the numbers one through ten, the words yes, no, and goodbye, along with all the letters of the alphabet. Parker Brothers, a major board game manufacturer patented the board and massed produced it in the late 1960s. I can still remember seeing the television commercials as a child.

"It must have been a happy day in Hell when that was introduced to the public," Sister stated. Because, in her view, the gates of the pit had been flung wide open and its minions given an open invitation to possess the unsuspecting users of this evil instrument advertised as a harmless pass-time.

"Is there anyone here who wishes to communicate with us?" I could hear the little Goth girl ask of no one.

"No," had apparently been the answer the oracle pointed to in response. I couldn't blame the spirits for not wanting to talk to this motley crew and I found the *no* reply to be somewhat amusing.

"Do you want us to leave?" The little Goth girl asked her next question.

"Yes," she repeated the answer the oracle glided to.

"Tell us your name," she commanded of the entity.

"W… I… T… C… H..." then "Goodbye," she called out the letters and the word as they were indicated by the oracle. It appeared this ghost could indeed spell. The séance was apparently over.

The spirits there didn't seem to think very highly of these witches and I was sure that their bad attitude towards the living had been also recognized by the dead. The words *reap what you have sown* suddenly sounded in my head and I didn't think they had been a random thought on my part. I wasn't sure who put them there… But I didn't think it could have been me.

~~~~~~~

"You've got mail," the voice on the computer alerted me. I glanced at the screen to see it was from my friend, Ryan, the night watchman at the prison.

'I can find nothing in the north gatehouse that could have explained the phantom face in your picture,' the email read. 'There are no stains on the wall or anything that could have been mistaken for what is present in your photo. Just an empty room,' he went on to say.

This was great validation for my new ghost picture and, of course, validation was what I sought. He ended the note with his congratulations on my capture of the phantom head. He also informed me he ordered himself a ghost radio off the internet. He was anxiously awaiting its arrival so he too could attempt to communicate with the spirits there in real time.

I wasn't even aware you could buy one of those online, but yes…indeed, you can. I replied to his email and thanked him for taking the time to verify there was no rational explanation for the anomaly in my photo.
~~~~~~~

CHAPTER TWENTY-TWO

Gabreael advised me to build a website for myself so others who may be seeking help would have a way to contact me. For others who perhaps experienced unexplained activity in their homes as I did… Or still do, rather. For someone who also questioned their own sanity and religious beliefs. The site would also be a great place for me to post the findings of my research, such as the pictures and my EVPs to share them with the world.

"Every honest ghost hunter should have a website," she stated.

I never even thought of the concept of my own website and had no idea where to begin.

"It's not hard to do, I'll help you get the site started," she assured me. "The first step is to think of a name for your website," she advised.

I didn't have to think long to come up with one as it seemed to come to mind instantly. I almost felt as if the name had been given to me by something outside my own consciousness.

Piedmontparanormalresearch.com is what the suggestion had been. From who or what, I was not sure. But research had to be included in the name. After all, research is what started this journey from which I knew there would be no turning back.

~~~~~~~

The spirits in my home seem to come and go. At times I could turn on the recorder or ghost radio and hardly get a voice or reply from them. Then, maybe the next day, they wouldn't shut up long enough for me to ask any questions.

"The bridges are moving," was the response I got when I asked where they had been. Could they have been referring to the portal here in my home? Did it open and close like some drawbridge from one side to the other? What if it closes when they are in this realm—in my living room? Is that why they were trapped here? And if this portal or bridge does open and close, what causes it? What controls it? Where does it lead? Will it lead one to the pearly gates, or just some place *in-between? Just more damn questions to ponder*.

~~~~~~~

I thought back on the trip to Moundsville. Were the inmates there held against their will, by some unseen force which acted as an eternal jailer? Trapped in that hell-hole by *something unseen*? Or were they simply the victims of their own beliefs—held in that place by their own worst fears? Whatever the reason, I was sure that, yes, they did indeed linger there in that abandoned place.

Could the demons Sister battled, such as the one I photographed in Asheville, have been a manifestation of Amelia's belief she must be punished for the sins of her past? I wasn't sure, but I did have the demonic looking face in my picture to ponder. *Fear the demons* had been the phantom words imprinted on my recorder at the graveyard. I took their advice and heeded them.

Was it our fear that manifested the shadow man in our home? I was sure he had been here. He appeared to Lynn on two occasions and I felt his dark presence in the attic that evening. I still feel it today, I was suddenly reminded, as my shoulder throbbed at the thought of that night.

Yes, I definitely believe these things do exist. I thought back on a Bible passage I read. I can't recall which one, but it spoke of Christ casting out demons from some afflicted men. I guess the young Pastor must have skipped that page.

So there, written in black and white, is mention of exactly what he claimed could not happen—demons influencing or possessing the living. Not according to the teachings of his doctrine, anyway. Nope, I am not of that faith anymore. The Catholics must have been paying closer attention, though, for they even appointed special priest to deal with the demonic entities that plagued their parishioners.

~~~~~~~

Your fear can't protect you, also a warning from beyond I recorded in my office on the night Lynn took her ghost walk. Did these dark beings feed on our fear? Was that the message? Was it fear that gave them power. Was it fear that manifested them?

Many of the spirits asked me for my help including those at the Moundsville prison. *Reap what you have sown,* again, inexplicably sounded in my head. "Okay, I think I understand," I said to no one. At least, I thought I was beginning to understand the voice inside my head.

Does a madman realize he is insane? The jury was still out on that one, but I thought maybe the message had to do with one's intent. What you put out comes back to you… Were they speaking of *karma*? If you put out hatred, like the coven members, then you will get hatred in return. If you believe in and fear something
~~~~~~~

negative, the fear and negativity will come back to you. If you believe you should be punished for your sins, such as Amelia, then you will be punished. If you send out good energy, such as the love for your fellow beings and a desire to help others, it will be returned to you. Whether they are living, or deceased, apparently.

If you love God and worship him, then the blessings will flow. If you curse Him, then God help you. *We cursed at God* had been the message from the cemetery when I asked why they lingered there. What I read from that EVP was because this spirit turned his back on God, God returned the favor and left him *in-between*. Maybe so he would have eternity to reflect on his actions? Or maybe, prayer for his soul was what he needed to free him from the prison. After all, the words *pray for me* had been the first request whispered on my camera audio—the three words that began all of my research as to who and why those words were spoken.

The thing that still has me perplexed is all the children I have contacted, especially, those in the cemetery. Why are they trapped there and what can I do to set them free? For if the kingdom of Heaven does belong to such as these, do they not belong with the angels? This question haunts me more than any other. Perhaps my research will one day yield the answers. Something must be holding them there in the stones–some dark force that prevents them from entering the light of heaven. Yes… *Something unseen.*

~~~~~~~

Gabreael called and invited me to be a guest on her radio show, *A Glimpse Through the Veil.*

"Me?" I asked her.

"Yes, Stephen," she replied. "You are a very gifted person and you have an incredible story to tell."

I couldn't argue with her on the last part of her statement, I did have quite a story to tell. But I could take no credit for the gift I was
~~~~~~~

blessed with at birth. For if it was from birth, it meant *from God* as far as I was concerned. So, to Him I must give all the glory.

I counted the days until her show was scheduled to be on. It was hosted by a paranormal/metaphysical internet network and was broadcast to the entire world. The thought of this made me a bit nervous, to say the least. Finally, the day arrived.

Gabreael shot me a quick email to tell me she would call at eight p.m. to begin the live broadcast. What if the world thinks I'm just a crazy old man? What if they don't believe what I have to tell them? I began to have second thoughts. Does a madman realize he is insane? Does he question his own sanity? Would her audience view me as the young Pastor had? I called her and voiced my concerns.

"Don't worry, Stephen, you'll do just fine. Just be yourself. It will be fun!"

For some reason, I didn't quite believe her. What if they did think I was crazy?

"I know you will do fine, Steve," she reassured me.

"Okay, I'll do it," I finally conceded. After all, knowing was her specialty.

"Good evening, everyone, and welcome to this week's edition of *A Glimpse Through the Veil*. I am Gabreael, your host, and tonight we will be talking with Mr. Stephen Hill. Steve comes to us as an Electronic Medium, founder of Piedmont Paranormal Research and also as a haunted homeowner. Steve, tell us what brought you into the field of paranormal research."

"Thank you for inviting me to be on your show. And that is a great question, Gabreael," I said as I wondered if the world could hear the nervousness in my voice. How many names would now be added to the list? Only one way to find out… I took a deep breath.

"There is an old saying that dates back from the pirate days and

I have heard it many times throughout my life. *Dead men tell no tales.* I always thought this saying to be logical and true. That is—until the day I accidentally discovered that sometimes they can and do. Speak—I mean. I didn't believe it myself at first, so I'll understand if you choose not to believe me now. If you think me insane, then it's okay, you won't be the first. At times I have thought so myself. But I want you to know that every word is true and it just might change your outlook on life—and death. Just as it has forever changed mine."

My world debut was then interrupted by a very cold, wet nose on my elbow. "Damn it, Cruzer!"

Made in the USA
Lexington, KY
23 October 2012